D1001933

THE SCIENCE AND CULTURE SERIES
REV. JOSEPH HUSSLEIN, S.J., PH.D., GENERAL EDITOR

PERSONALITY
AND
SUCCESSFUL LIVING

PERSONALITY AND SUCCESSFUL LIVING

By

JAMES A. MAGNER
The Catholic University of America

THE BRUCE PUBLISHING COMPANY
Milwaukee

Nihil obstat: H. B. Ries, Censor librorum
Imprimatur: ✠ Moses E. Kiley, Archbishop of Milwaukee
December 16, 1944

(Fourth Printing – 1946)

Gratefully Dedicated to
a Loyal Friend
Simon A. Baldus

Grateful acknowledgment is made to the editors of *Ave Maria* and *The Sign* for permission to reproduce certain materials herein; also to other publishers, as indicated, for permission to quote from various authors.

PREFACE BY THE GENERAL EDITOR

THE art of successful living" is the expression aptly used by the author, at the conclusion of his book, to designate the subject treated by him. For what else is the cultivation of a Christian Personality than the development of a perfect life; a life exquisitely balanced, of good repute and noble service to our neighbor; a life most happily modeled on Christ Himself.

There are few words in the entire lexicon so rich in meaning as that one term, "Personality." In a single breath it expresses all we are in soul and body – the total man, as one might say. Yet at the same time it serves no less to distinguish each individual from every other in the universe when we come to speak of his *own* personality, of the combination of traits and qualities that characterize him.

It is by our personality, therefore, that men judge us in society, and according to which they assign to us the place we hold in their esteem. No little, therefore, of psychological insight is required in the treatment of this subject: in probing false motives, detecting devious reasonings and unraveling our own cunning self-deceptions.

Indeed, an Everyman's Psychology, this book might not improperly be called, but a psychology that is practical, popular, and always kept on the familiar level of everyday experience.

Natural motives are duly stressed by the author and never overlooked, yet without prejudice to the supernatural, to which supreme consideration must evidently be given. Love of the neighbor for the love of God is the true Christian motivation of all social service.

Yet it is not from the standpoint of a recluse that this book is written, but from that of a man immersed in the absorbing business of daily experience with money, men, and ledgers. Not of least value to us also are his fertile reminiscences of childhood and schoolboy days, kept strikingly vivid and fresh, while with seeing eyes he views in the world about him the passing pageant of trials and triumphs, of failures and successes in the social drama. Ulysses-like, he is part of much at least of all that he describes.

It is precisely, then, this living interest in things, events and persons which makes of his book a practical aid for the proper development of self, and a safe rule for the guidance of others whom Providence may entrust to our care.

Illustrations gathered from personal experience, and citations gleaned from literature abound in its pages, while all familiar fields are more or less touched upon: the home, the school, society, democracy, business, employment, stocks and bonds, and whatever else can well enter into the range of ordinary human experience. Never is our interest allowed to lag.

Cultural development of personality, mental and spiritual, is not achieved over night. It is the result of much thought and insight, of careful planning and above all of diligent, devoted and prayerful daily patterning upon

Christ, the Divine Model, who Himself "advanced in wisdom, and age and grace with God and man."*

In that simple text, describing the youthful Christ on his return from the Temple, when already at the Jewish legal age for citizenship, we have the finest of all descriptions of growth in personality under the all-seeing eye of Heaven and the daily observation of men. It is the ideal here proposed to us.

JOSEPH HUSSLEIN, S.J., PH.D.
General Editor, Science and Culture Series

St. Louis University,
April 25, 1944.

* Luke 2:52.

SHORT LIST OF SUGGESTED READING

Allers, Rudolph: *Psychology of Character,* Trans. Strauss, new ed., Sheed and Ward, New York, 1943.

—— *Character Education in Adolescence,* J. F. Wagner, New York, 1940.

—— *Self-Improvement,* Benziger Bros., New York, 1939.

Carroll, Robert S.: *The Mastery of Nervousness,* Macmillan, New York, 1918.

Burnham, W. H.: *The Normal Mind,* Appleton, New York, 1924.

—— *The Wholesome Personality,* Appleton, New York, 1932.

Fosdick, Henry: *On Being a Real Person,* Harper, New York, 1943.

Lindworsky, John: *Training of the Will,* Bruce, Milwaukee, 1938.

McCarthy, R. C.: *Safeguarding Mental Health,* Bruce, Milwaukee, 1937.

Magner, James A.: *For God and Democracy,* Macmillan, New York, 1940.

Moore, T. V.: *Personal Mental Hygiene,* Grune and Stratton, New York, 1944.

Walsh, James J.: *Religion and Health,* Little, Brown and Co., Boston, 1920.

A valuable annotated list of books applicable to the character problems of children in the elementary grades and on the high school level has been compiled by:

Kircher, Clara J.: *Character Formation Through Books: A Bibliography*. The Catholic University of America Press, Washington, 2nd ed., 1945.

CONTENTS

CHAPTER 1

THE MEANING OF CHRISTIAN PERSONALITY

"I am the Way, the Truth, and the Life. No man cometh to the Father, but by Me" (John 14:6).

I

"TO BE honest," said the great poet Goethe shortly before the last review, "what did I possess that was really my own, beyond the capacity and inclination to see and hear . . . and render with some skill? I owe my achievements . . . to thousands of things and persons outside myself, which constituted my material. Fools and sages, clear-brained men and narrow-minded men, children and young people, to say nothing of ripe seniors – they all came to me, all told me how things struck them . . . and all I had to do was to catch hold of it, and reap what others had sown for me. . . . The main thing is to have a great desire, and skill and perseverance to accomplish it. . . . My work is that of a composite being . . ."[1]

There can be no doubt that we are highly composite

[1] Emil Ludwig, *Goethe* (New York: G. P. Putnam's Sons, 1928), pp. 637–638.

beings, reproducing the traits not of our parents only, but often of some strange and unknown ancestor of the past, reflecting the forgotten impressions of childhood, and combining the various influences of all, both good and bad, with whom we have come in contact. Many of these influences play upon us despite our determination to avoid them. I have known students, for example, to conceive a bitter dislike for certain teachers and in particular for their mannerisms, only to acquire these self-same characteristics and even to reproduce the mentality they hated.

Somehow, all of it, even the wounds of experience, becomes a part of us and helps to shape our outlook on ourselves, the world, and the future ahead. As Ulysses declared, in the poem of Tennyson:

> I am a part of all that I have met;
> Yet all experience is an arch wherethro'
> Gleams that untravell'd world whose margin fades
> For ever and for ever when I move.[2]

There are moments when each of us wonders just what kind of person he should have been had he been reared in different circumstances, or in another country, had he possessed better or worse educational opportunities, or had he not been confronted with certain problems. This thought has often come to me when in a crowd of strangers some face or voice stands out as strikingly reminiscent of someone I know, or when, as is frequently the case, I am mistaken for someone else.

Be this as it may, however, we are by no means slaves of our environment nor are we limited by the opportunities of any particular moment. The human personality is not simply a "stream of consciousness" flowing on through different landscapes. It is not simply a mirror

---

[2] Alfred Lord Tennyson, *Ulysses*.

reflecting different scenes and persons and letting them go forever. It is not even a bundle of complexes behaving uniformly as the impulses of nature or chemistry or "nerves" command.

There is in every one of us an abiding principle of intelligence and of free will endowed with the power to command. This principle is a spiritual substance or soul united to the body, making the composition which we call human nature, by which we act. The human person is, therefore, a complete and substantial unit of operation, independent in itself, incapable of being diminished or shared by any other person, and exercising as a responsible being the activity over which it has control. It is precisely because a man is endowed with this conscious and independent intelligence that he is a person. This distinguishes him from the brutes or irrational animals. Some men may look like monkeys, and some monkeys may look like men; but the monkey, lacking a rational soul, is not a person, cannot be said to have a personality, in the strict and true sense of the word, and has no rights or duties, as we understand them in a moral sense.

In a wider sense, personality designates not only the essential composition of body and soul but also the whole individual who acts. It embraces his appearance, his manners, his habits, his likes and dislikes — everything, in fact, that can be ascribed to him. We say, for example, that so-and-so has a pleasing personality, in other words that he or she walks or converses or reacts to situations in a gracious and agreeable manner. The tone of the voice, the sparkle of wit, the natural poise and animation of the individual, and a thousand other external indications, help us to identify and classify a person, for the reason that, although they are only passing manifestations, they point out the qualities of the abiding or permanent soul of the individual.

For this reason, the perfection of one's personality may well be judged in part by such items as beauty of features and proportions of the body, neatness, bearing, and even, in a participated sense, by taste in dress and general physical charm and attractiveness. From this standpoint, we often say that one is careful or careless of his person. We recognize also that there is something which we may designate, for lack of a better understanding, as animal magnetism that makes some persons more likeable than others or makes a particular appeal to certain individuals, without adequate explanation. It is probably this element, or this combination of elements that causes particular men and women to fall in love with each other rather than with different persons of the opposite sex. Contrariwise, it probably has a good deal to do with repelling others, whether of the same or of the opposite sex.

There are some persons whom we find it almost impossible to like, even though they have never injured us and are, so far as we know, quite admirable in themselves. In the words of the old jingle, we find ourselves frequently saying:

> I do not like thee, Dr. Fell,
> The reason why, I cannot tell.

On the other hand, we all have had the experience of meeting the same persons after an interval of years, to find that either they or we have changed very agreeably. All this indicates that there are in the human personality, even in its lower and less important phases, variable elements which are capable of improvement.

It is said that St. Francis de Sales desired his flock to be the best dressed people of the community, and indeed there is no reason why one should neglect those external and often intangible touches in one's appearance. Most spiritual writers, dealing with the personality of Christ, are agreed that He was handsome and striking in appearance; and while we are told that He was a poor man, so far as financial resources are concerned, the Christian mind, as expressed in art, generally represents Him as neat, appropriately clothed, and well groomed.

In a sheerly materialistic and pagan conception of personality, it is possible to overemphasize the importance of one's physical appearance and external grace. Manufacturers of beauty preparations, particularly for women, often go to ridiculous lengths to make it appear that mastery of oneself and of the world's treasures lies in a perfume bottle. On the other hand, some of the saints, we are told, went to the opposite extreme, neglecting their personal appearance altogether, and even disfigured themselves in an effort to flee the temptations of vanity. Nevertheless, the average individual cannot do better, in laying the foundations for a healthy and great personality, than to recognize the value of a sound body and an agreeable presentation of his physical appearance as a symbol of a sound mind and rational sense of moral values.

"That Jesus did not close His heart to the joys of mankind," writes Karl Adam, "that He was not like the Baptist a man of the desert, clothed in a garment of camel's hair, whose meat was locusts and wild honey; that He went among people in every day garb, a 'cloak without seam' (John 19:23) adorned with hems (Matt.

14:35); that He took part quite naturally in their festivities and merrymakings so that His enemies taunted Him with being a 'glutton and a wine-drinker' (Matt. 11:19); that He did not hesitate to work His first miracle to please the guests at a marriage feast; that He would not have His disciples fast so long as the bridegroom was with them (Matt. 2:19); that He held one of His followers very dear and let him lean on His bosom (John 13:23); and lastly that the whole of this exhuberant vitality was set in a frame so full of charm and grace and loveliness, that in it alone we cannot fail to recognize a great, a supremely great poet, who with a unique creative touch makes the whole of nature live for us – the fig-trees and the lilies, the mustard trees and the vines, the sparrow and the fox, the glad sunshine and the wild tempest; all this betrays such a generosity, openness of heart, breadth and responsiveness and tenderness and delicacy of spirit as has no counterpart in any heroic or strictly ascetical nature."[3]

II

It is important to notice, as Karl Adam indicated, that the abiding qualities as well as the real source of Christ's physical beauty and external qualities as well as charm come from the greatness and beauty of His inner personality. This experience is repeated so often that we understand perfectly what is meant. A pleasing exterior without corresponding moral qualities is inevitably disappointing. Women may spend hours before the mirror without improving their personality one

---

[3] *The Son of God* (New York: Sheed and Ward, 1934), pp. 131, 132.

whit; and men may develop the most exquisite manners and faultless wardrobes only to discover, if they have the comprehension to discover, that they are in the class known as "stuffed shirts." On the other hand, many of the most delightful people we know are comparatively unattractive in appearance and frequently disappointing at first sight. To visualize people by the books they write, or by their radio voice, or by their achievements, or by the reputation which precedes them, may be quite misleading. The tall, handsome, fascinating creature we have built in our mind's eye may turn out to be a very plain person indeed; but if the inner qualities are there, we soon come to forget our original specifications and succumb to the human influence and cultural or spiritual charm of the individual.

Inasmuch as personality is really the individualization of one's spiritual nature, it is quite natural that this should be the right order of importance. Moreover, while no one, as Christ says, "by taking thought can add to his stature one cubit," it is within our power to modify, change, develop, and perfect our attitudes of mind, our emotional reactions, and the habits that fall under the competence of our wills. These habits and developed aptitudes are what make up character and integrate personality.

When we speak of Christian personality, therefore, we are thinking in terms of a conscious development along the lines of private and social conduct as taught and practised by Christ. "How then," asks Karl Adam, whose book I earnestly recommend, "did Jesus behave as a simple human being? What idea are we to have of His purely human mental disposition? The Evangelists give us unequivocal information on this point.

What struck them most in His human nature and what they were always underlining was the tremendous clarity of His thought, the sure consciousness He had of His aim, and the resultant inflexibility and finality of His will."[4] And again, "the purposeful virility, the absolute genuineness, the austere uprightness, in a word the heroic in the personality of Jesus, is the first thing in His human nature to strike the eye of the psychologist."[5]

For the reason that the principles of life delivered by Christ are so clean-cut and come within the executive force of every human will, they offer a rule and pattern of human development that must create a distinctive type of personality. What we may refer to as Christian poise and maturity are the result of education both in the grasp of Christian principle as applied to one's life and in the exercise of a purposeful will easily and spontaneously carrying out the rational decisions of a Christian mind.

This conception of personal development also gives us a true insight into the meaning of sanctity. Sanctity is not merely a mechanical avoidance of or flight from those attitudes or actions technically called sins. Much less is it a sort of queer accomplishment, like walking barefoot over sharp nails or heroically denying oneself the normal forms of human joy and intercourse. It is rather a complete and integral growth of mind and will, a rational development and activity of all one's powers in appreciation of the purpose of existence, which is to recognize God in the beauty of His creation, to know, love, and serve Him, and to share His creative activity by service to one's fellow men.

---

[4] Karl Adam, *op. cit.*, p. 94.
[5] *Op. cit.*, p. 105.

There is a mistaken idea that saints are erratic persons, difficult to live with. If people are difficult to live with, the fault is either in their shortcomings or in our own; and in the same proportion there is a definite lack of sanctity on either side. The difficulty very often is that the terms "sanctity" and "religion" are tacked to an external display or reputation of performing certain acts of worship or of abiding by certain religious observances. In the same way, "saving one's soul" is frequently interpreted as taking time out of one's life to reach a friendly understanding or gentleman's agreement with God. The formation of character, the development of personality, growth in sanctity, genuine religion, and saving one's soul, however, are all phases of one and the same thing. As soon as one or the other is set off into a separate compartment, a warping process takes place.

In the words of St. Paul: "If I speak with the tongues of men and of angels, and have not charity, I am become as sounding brass, or a tinkling cymbal. And if I should have prophecy and should know all mysteries, and all knowledge, and if I should have all faith, so that I could remove mountains, and have not charity, I am nothing. And if I should distribute all my goods to feed the poor, and if I should deliver my body to to be burned, and have not charity, it profiteth me nothing."[6]

Another error which has given rise to a distorted conception of sanctity is that this world is a kind of prison house and that if one can only endure it long enough, without trying to rebel or tasting its illusory pleasures, one will suddenly be ushered, in the next

[6] 1 Cor. 13:1–3.

life, into glory which will compensate for what he has missed here below. It is true that, in His Beatitudes, Christ holds out a heavenly reward for all who suffer in this life for the sake of justice. It is also true that He laid the lash of strong words on those who content themselves with the enjoyment of this world's goods, that in His instructions to the young man who was seeking perfection, He said: "If thou wilt be perfect, go sell what thou hast and give to the poor and thou shalt have treasure in heaven. And come follow me."[7] But it is important to remember that He cast into exterior darkness the unprofitable servant who buried his talents in a napkin, instead of investing them gainfully, and that He shut out the five foolish virgins who failed to keep oil in their lamps for the bridal party.[8] And even while upbraiding those who think exclusively of what they shall eat and of what they shall put on; and while asking "Is not the life more than the meat, and the body more than the raiment?" – He pointed out that God takes care even of the lilies of the field and the birds of the air.[9]

Christ's view of life was by no means a mournful one. Even upon the Cross, indeed most upon the Cross, He held out hope for mankind and gave each individual a rational faith in himself and in the high purpose of his existence. What He constantly stressed was that the most important values should be given first consideration and that everything else would then fall in line. "Seek ye first the kingdom of God and his justice," He said, indicating that perfection and happiness lie in the

---

[7] Matt. 19:21.
[8] Matt. 25:1–13.
[9] Matt. 6:25–34.

union of our powers with the mind of God, "and all these things shall be added unto you."[10]

This by no means indicates that one should simply take himself for what he is, satisfied with mediocrity and contemptuous of material improvement or cultural advance. As a child, "Jesus advanced in wisdom and age, and grace with God and men."[11] There is no reason to suppose that this development stopped as soon as He reached adulthood. Indeed, if God's glory is manifested in the right use of intelligence, it seems only reasonable that the capacities of the individual to enjoy the contemplation of God in the next life should be at least somewhat proportionate to their development in this life. Persons who imagine that salvation is a matter of technicalities, to be achieved by putting a compression on their generous emotions, despising cultural appreciation, closing all doors on human relationships, and meriting a ticket to the galleries of heaven by closing their eyes to the beauty of God as revealed in this world, may have a rude awakening to their meanness and poverty of spirit on the threshold of Eternity.

It is true that moral merit is based essentially on endeavor, which is properly an activity of the will; and in this respect all persons, whether of high or low degree, of greater or less talent, are equal in the face of judgment at the throne of God. Nevertheless, even in terms of the immortality of the soul, it seems hardly plausible that the capacities of the soul to enjoy merit are enlarged simply by a desire for salvation and a careful avoidance of technical sin. The powers of the

---

[10] Matt. 6:33.
[11] Luke 2:52.

will must be expressed, not in a series of cautious negations, but in a constant constructive and affirmative activity, following the indications of an alert mind to which the existence and the attributes of God are unfolded increasingly day by day.

III

This conception of personality and of its development are in thorough accord with the principles also of supernatural grace and with the growth in grace, as revealed by Christ. Thus, He declared, "I am the true vine: and my Father is the true husbandman. Every branch in me that beareth not fruit, he will take away: and every one that beareth fruit, he will purge it, that it may bring forth more fruit. . . . Abide in me: and I in you. As the branch cannot bear fruit of itself, unless it abide in the vine, so neither can you, unless you abide in me."[12]

Wonderful though this divine assistance is, mysterious in its supernatural operation, and completely gratuitous on the part of God, it is nevertheless proportioned to the disposition of the individual who receives it and is increased as the person freely avails himself of it. "He that is just, let him be justified still," declared the author of the Apocalypse, "and he that is holy, let him be sanctified still."[13] And St. Peter wrote: "Grow in grace, and in the knowledge of our Lord and Saviour Jesus Christ."[14]

The special glory of a truly Christian personality, therefore, is this union through grace with God. "God is charity," according to St. John: "and he that abideth

---

[12] John 15:1-4.
[13] Apoc. 22:11.
[14] 2 Peter 3:18.

in charity abideth in God, and God in him."[15] With the same vision of eternal truth, St. Paul asked: "Know you not that you are the temple of God, and that the Spirit of God dwelleth in you?"[16] It is clear that divine revelation proposes a conception of individual dignity immeasurably more sublime than anything which reason alone has been able to devise.

This does not mean that the individual becomes merely a puppet in God's hands. On the contrary, the supernatural life of grace is infused into the soul and accompanies conscious activity, without in the least diminishing its responsibility or freedom. "Draw nigh to God," said St. James, "and He will draw nigh to you."[17] The old adage, "Pray as if everything depended on God, and work as if everything depended on yourself," is good Christian psychology.

It is true that occasionally the infusion of grace comes almost as a torrent and revolutionizes a personality almost instantaneously; but this is indeed rare. St. Paul described his own experience when, about to persecute the Christians at Damascus, he was thrown blind from his horse by the Lord and converted on the spot.[18] The novelist J. K. Huysmans, whose return to the Catholic faith was a sensation of his day, wrote a somewhat similar experience. "Only little by little," he declared, "I was shaking myself loose from my shell of impurity; I was beginning to have a disgust of myself, but at the same time I kicked against the articles of the Faith. The objections I raised in my own mind seemed irresistible; and lo! one fine morning when I woke

---

[15] 1 John 4:16.
[16] 1 Cor. 3:16.
[17] James 4:8.
[18] Acts 9.

they were solved – I never knew how. I prayed for the first time, and the catastrophe was over.

"For such as do not believe in the grace of God, all this seems folly. For those who have experienced its effects, no surprise is possible; or, if surprise there were, it could continue only over the period of incubation, the period when one sees nothing and notices nothing, the period of the clearing of the ground and laying of the foundations of which one never had even a suspicion."[19]

It is interesting to note that these lines of Huysmans were written in 1903, after his conversion and fourteen years after the appearance of the volume to which they served as a postscript. The closing lines of that terrible volume expressed the confusion of a soul in the darkness of night just before the dawn: "Lord," he cried, "take pity on the Christian who doubts, on the skeptic who would fain believe, on the galley-slave of life who puts out to sea alone, in the darkness of night, beneath a firmament illumined no longer by the consoling beacon-fires of the ancient hope."[20]

There can be no doubt that what often appears as the miracle of sudden grace really represents a long series of hidden promptings of divine grace. From a sheerly natural standpoint, the development of Christian character is likewise the product, not of a sudden and disconnected impulse, but rather of a long and gradual preparation. The outlooks and experiences of childhood, the influence and example of one's elders and childhood heroes, the principles picked up from

---

[19] J. K. Huysmans, *Against the Grain* (New York: Illustrated Editions Co., 1931), Introduction, pp. 71–72.
[20] *Op. cit.*, p. 339.

formal education, fleeting impressions and experiences – all go to prepare the mind and shape the will, subconsciously if you will or at least insensibly, to the full flowering of personality.

It is the right combination of these elements, first in the discipline that is imposed upon us and later in the deliberate choice of habits and of other psychological factors under our command, that helps us to become the men and women that we wish to be. Christian standards and Christian values are easily learned. Their application is a matter of daily self-examination and of effort in the concrete circumstances in which we find ourselves. Attention to the details of conduct and a consciousness of the items which in particular we must aim at are essential, if we are determined to perfect ourselves in the pattern of Christ and reach something of the goodness and grandeur of His human nature governed by His divine Personality.

CHAPTER 2

DEVELOPING SELF-CONFIDENCE

"And he that taketh not up his cross, nor followeth Me, is not worthy of Me" (Matt. 10:38).

I

ONE of the very first problems in the development of Christian personality is a true evaluation of self. In many ways we all deceive ourselves, finding false reasons to cover up dubious lines of action, adopting mental poses to harden ourselves in a justification of unconventional situations, and allowing our general outlooks to be colored by isolated experiences.

It is, of course, much easier to deceive ourselves than to deceive others. The much maligned ostrich serves to illustrate the point, although the story that he buries his head in the sand to hide himself from his enemies, I have been given to understand, is quite unscientific. Perhaps we had better see *ourselves* represented in the alleged rôle of the ostrich and recognize the fact that sincerity with self, although no easy task, is our best protection. Indeed it is the only solid foundation of character and final success.

The general error of self-deceit was recognized by Longfellow in his *Psalm of Life,* when he wrote:

> Tell me not in mournful numbers
> Life is but an empty dream,
> For the soul is dead that slumbers,
> And things are not what they seem.

This is so true that one may frequently arrive at the truth of things by studying their opposites. There is no doubt that a great deal of crusading self-assertion and feverish activity is due to a profound sense of spiritual confusion. The blatant shouting of dictators is but a reflection of their inner terror, like that of a whistler as he passes the midnight graveyard. The wars that are making the earth run red are an open proof of desperate cowardice in men and nations that are afraid to solve their common problems on the basis of reason and justice. On the other hand, human ambition, if it rises from the wellsprings of genuine confidence in self as a child of God and friend of mankind, brings forth the fruit of noble living and constructive action.

It may be true that some persons are born with a natural mental poise that makes the problem of self-adjustment and evaluation a minor matter. A well-balanced estimate of oneself and of one's powers is indeed a gift, if it comes easily. But for the most of us, the experience of dejection, discouragement, and timidity toward life represents a major and constant struggle in one form or the other. It may show itself in a general sense of being alone, of being unequal to life's requirements, or it may go on to assert itself in the conviction of having been given a bad deal or a series of bad deals. This is to state the issue very simply. In its human ramifications and results, this shrinking from life may become extremely complex.

A number and variety of causes can be assigned for

the difficulty. Some are sheerly external. The weather and climatic conditions have a profound effect upon all living creatures. Damp, heavy days have a way of driving birds to shelter; their songs are saved for sunny weather. Extreme heat and cold have a direct bearing on human energies, and, if prolonged, can produce wide modifications of temperament. Ambitious northerners, who like to despise the more leisurely inhabitants of the tropics, can easily change their outlook on activity after a few weeks under a blazing sun.

The same is true of one's internal physical conditions or state of health. An upset stomach, a nervous condition produced, let us say, by a goiter, or low vitality and anemia can radically affect one's mental outlook, temporarily or permanently, depending on the nature of the ailment. To keep a cheerful disposition and optimistic philosophy of life is no easy task when one is wracked with pain. Indeed, one's health can come to dominate life. People who are not well often spend most of their remaining energy speaking of their ailments and allowing their friends to share in the luxury of miserable feeling.

It is important to recognize the influence of physical states and to attempt to master the situation on this basis. If, for example, I find that common colds have a depressing effect on my mind, I must learn to attach no importance to the sudden suspicions or ugly thoughts that plague me during this period. When my vitality is low, or my physical system is agitated, I must avoid making judgments or deciding on important courses of action that I may later regret when my normal outlook returns.

In the development of the body from childhood,

through adolescence, on to maturity, and later in the subsiding of the reproductive faculties on the threshold of postmaturity, there is a corresponding nervous strain. It is important to recognize the physiological nature of this strain, if one is to apply rational mental controls. The same is true during the recurrent periods of physical climax in maturity. During such times, women particularly are subject to fits of melancholy and nervous brooding. If one could learn from experience that states of mental depression coincide with these periods, and that they have little or no bearing upon the real nature of external facts, one might be spared many a humiliating experience of brash temper or hasty action. During such periods, the best policy is to pay little attention to what one thinks about life and to observe the golden rule of silence when tempted to complaint or strong expression. Plenty of rest and relaxation may also be prescribed as helpful.

It is impossible to place too much stress on the necessity of avoiding excessive fatigue and of getting sufficient rest. The fast pace of modern life – late hours, hard work and hard play, immoderate indulgence in alcoholic drinks and in smoking – take a terrific toll. The result shows itself in a thousand ways: by inefficiency in work, frequent accidents, lowered resistance to disease, mental depression, ragged nerves, and bad dispositions. It is probable that more sins against charity in word and deed are committed as the result of insufficient sleep, than from any other single cause. The principal reasons why Monday is called "blue" are overindulgence over the week end and late hours on Sunday night. Most people dislike going to bed at night and equally dislike arising in the morning. One must learn to put aside the book or the newspaper at a reasonable hour, and one must discipline his social calendar of evening activities to correspond with the requirements of his waking hours. Because of a disregard of these fundamental considerations, a large number of people pass most of their lives in a partial daze.

II

The psychological problem to be dealt with, however, may be far deeper than indicated on the surface and may find its roots in a chronic, almost constitutional discouragement. The feeling of inferiority and failure plagues many a person throughout life and sounds the note of defeat even before tasks are begun. Such a complex may easily develop from the experiences of childhood and of struggling youth, so that persons who are responsible for the formation of character frequently have a number of serious questions to ask themselves.

Every form of attention and adulation is showered upon infancy and early childhood. As a result, we are all ushered upon the threshold of consciousness under the delightful impression that we are the most wonderful creatures that have yet been born, and we come to look upon others as created for the sole purpose of ministering to our needs. Then comes the gradual awakening and disillusionment. We soon discover that we are in competition with others. We are frequently neglected and even rebuked. We are called upon to make our own decisions and to suffer the consequences of our follies. The day soon comes when we have to weep in a corner alone; and our passionate sobbing serves only to harden the stony hearts of our parents and elders.

These early years are extremely impressionable, and sometimes apparently inconsequential incidents leave a mark that remains long after important experiences of adulthood have been forgotten. A dear old lady once confided to me, almost in a whisper, that all her life she had been afraid of churches, because as a little girl she had one day been reprimanded by her pastor for walking on his newly sodded lawn. Claustrophobia and similar forms of fear are often the result of an unfortunate experience in childhood.

Particular difficulties arise during the period of adolescence, those hobbledehoy years, when boys begin to walk and talk like men and girls begin to wonder whether they are really understood by their parents. These are years of fantastic dreams and confused thinking, but they represent the emergence of personality, and they call for real understanding and companionship. The difficulty with many parents is that they can hardly realize that their boys and girls are rapidly attaining maturity, with ideas and tremendous problems of their own. Older brothers and sisters find it difficult to change their superior attitudes, to stop their incessant banter, and to begin a companionship with the younger members of the family on a serious basis. As a teacher of boys, with an occasional tendency to register contempt for what might appear to be only a vegetable consciousness on their part, I have frequently been obliged to remind myself that at this selfsame age I was a thinking and deeply sensitive machine, with ideas of my own and a sense of personal dignity which could be easily wounded or properly respected.

Adolescents struggling for a foothold in life, young men and women striving to adjust themselves in their first occupation, all need the assistance of appreciative and considerate friends. Rebuffs, neglect, and failure to be taken seriously at this stage may easily engender an outlook of mistrust, disconfidence, and fear toward life. If, in addition, the youth labors under the impression that he lacks the necessary talents or qualifications to make his way in life, the results may be disastrous.

For this reason, it is of the greatest consequence that young men and women should have at least a general idea of the lines upon which their talents lie, at least some conception of what they should like to do, and some inspiring interest to help them reach their goal and to realize their ambitions. Most boys, at an early age, decide that they are going to be policemen, or firemen, or to engage in some thrilling pursuit; but by the time they are ready to win their own bread, very few have any definite preparation or decision for a particular career. Most first "jobs" are secured by a combination of circumstances, and thereafter the career of the individual shapes itself by opportunity or accident. As a result, the world is full of misfits and of disgruntled persons whose ideas of work and of a life purpose are without co-ordination or clear definition.

It is a pity that there should not be more friendly counsel, a more personal interest in the qualifications of students by their teachers. Perhaps more specific differentiations in the curricula of our schools could do a great deal toward vocational direction. Fortunate indeed is the student who knows what he wants and works toward it.

If one cannot conceive a love for his work, life is indeed a drudgery. In fact, nothing great is done except through love. And for this, one must have at least a general knowledge of where his interests and powers lie and find in this an inspiration to achievement. Toward this objective, a careful selection of inspirational reading can provide a valuable impulse, even though it succeeds only in stimulating a general ambition. I can recall, as a boy, spending long hours devouring the inspirational books of Samuel Smiles and following the careers of the heroes whom he adduced as examples of determination and success. These works may seem antiquated today, but they served a useful purpose.

The desire of people for this kind of impulse today is amply demonstrated by the phenomenal success of such books as Dale Carnegie's *How to Win Friends and Influence People* and Walter Pitkin's *Life Begins at Forty*. So, too, I have seen people literally hanging from the rafters to hear the inspirational lectures of such men as Albert de Quevedo, coming back time and again to hear them and from their lips to learn an answer to their quest for the purpose of life. In times past, the lives of the saints were offered for pious reading. People today are willing to read the lives of the saints if they are presented factually. They are looking, not for pious consolation, but for practical guidance.

III

At this point, one may mention another source of mental confusion and distress, namely, that which arises from an unsolved moral problem or an agitated conscience. The conscience, as indicating the difference between right and wrong and pointing out the path of duty, is a department or function of the mind. It cannot be wounded or maltreated without affecting one's mental health. Those who attempt to disregard the danger signals and to reconstruct for themselves a moral code which is clearly in opposition to what they know, or strongly suspect, to be the true one must be prepared to suffer the consequences.

Some persons get off to a bad start in life. Either because of a supersensitive conscience or because of the overrigorous teaching of their parents, they may come, on the threshold of the age of reason, to regard every little misdemeanor and many innocent things as crimes against heaven, opening wide the jaws of hell. When native common sense becomes thus warped and at war with itself, the interior conflict can become serious. Later on, during the growing years, come the first mysterious movements of sex; and unless the child then meets his problems squarely, by taking counsel or receiving it from competent and tactful sources, the mind as well as the body can become the prey of a thousand disorders.

Some consciences are never at ease, for the reason that they find it difficult to come to a rational decision for themselves and to abide by that decision. Others fail to achieve peace, either because they have a shifting sense of values or because they attempt to build up a good case for their malodorous actions. The result in many cases is a rebellious attitude against established principles and a cynical or hypercritical attitude toward religion and established principles of morality. There is no doubt that many persons lose their religious faith, not because of intellectual difficulties but because of their inner conflict on a moral issue which they have solved by refusing to make a frank acknowledgment of personal guilt.

One of the shortcomings and profound errors of materialistic psychoanalysis is precisely that it ignores this element of moral accountability. Mental aberrations may sometimes be explained in the light of unfortunate or unusual experiences, but if a moral issue is involved, the mere uncovering of the secret sore will not solve the problem. There must also be a frank, courageous admission of sin and a hearty repentance, with the determination to avoid the evil in the future. Catholics have been instructed as to the meaning of moral delinquency in terms of accountability to Almighty God, and they have been provided with the sacrament of penance for a full and free reconciliation through contrite confession. Others, outside the Catholic faith, still have an obligation of reconciling themselves with God when evil has been done, and unless, with God's grace, this obligation is performed to the best of their honest ability, they can hardly expect mental peace or personal confidence.

In an altogether different category, but productive of various phobias and forms of chronic hesitancy, is prolonged idleness. One of the most harmful things that can happen to a boy or girl after completion of school is to remain without a definite occupation or responsibility. Until one learns to test himself in real action, he has not found what he is or what he can do. The longer we postpone our entry into real life, the more helpless we become and the more difficult the decision to act.

The longer one remains inactive, the more sluggish one's mental equipment becomes, and the more one consequently becomes subject to various hallucinations. The thrill goes out of life with idleness, and if the victim does not lapse into a complete loss of ambition, he frequently begins to imagine that the world is in a conspiracy against him. When idleness is combined with solitude, even more serious deterioration can result. Special forms of eccentricity develop, not only in mannerisms but in mental outlooks.

There is wisdom in the assertion that if a man remains out of work and manages to keep alive in New York City for one year, he will never work again. Many an enemy of society, for whose hands the devil finds work to do, can trace his first irregular impulses to a succession of idle moments.

One does not have to go to these lengths to find the evidences of a defeatist attitude toward life. The most common symptom is a spirit of general dissatisfaction. In itself, dissatisfaction with a particular group of circumstances is nothing to be alarmed about. On the contrary, it may indicate an alert and ambitious spirit that refuses to be weighed down by mediocrity or to be satisfied with a bad situation. But there are some people for whom dissatisfaction is a normal activity with reference to no particular objective. They are the constant complainers, for whom there is no justice or equity in the world, and whose spirits are congenial only in an atmosphere of discontent. Such discontent may be, and generally is, quite out of relation and proportion to facts.

There is, of course, a congenital disposition to complaint and psychological bolshevism among certain individual workers of all classes. Nothing suits them. Every concession is but the stepping stone to new grievances. The motives of superiors are always to be distrusted, in this mentality.

This cynical outlook, which sees the whole world as a "fake," goes one step beyond mere complaint, and, if sufficiently indulged, can pulverize all positive activity for the unhappy victim. "Why do you suppose so-and-so sent me that Christmas card or left that box of candy on my desk?" we say, looking for ulterior and evil motives in the kind deeds of others. Or, "so-and-so has been particularly pleasant today. There must be something wrong." Perhaps there may be a reason occasionally for this suspicion, but a constant disposition to look for the fly in the ointment can ruin all the goodness there is in life.

Occasionally mental confusion of this general type takes refuge in what I have already referred to as a "persecution complex." By this device, a person can explain his own shortcomings in terms of various conspiracies against him. Thus he can make himself believe that further effort is useless, since he is blocked at every turn by evil and designing persons or by unseen forces that make it impossible for him to get ahead. "The 'breaks,'" people sometimes say, "are all against me." To run away from reality, under the terror of these ghosts, men sometimes find their consolation in drink; and women, developing a sort of "God help us" voice, in the familiar rôle of Zazu Pitts, begin to regale every acquaintance with a recital of the indignities they are made to suffer. This can neither attract friends nor bring lasting relief. When persons say, "I wish I were dead," others are frequently tempted to agree that it might be a relief.

These various attitudes toward life, like all over-simplifications, are hardly more than poses which poorly conceal an inner void and sense of personal insecurity. They are but a few of the manifestations that might be multiplied for individual study. I often wonder whether stubborn people, for example, are aware that what they are exhibiting is, not strength, but weakness. And what shall we say of those who allow themselves to be brought into the position of a clown or funny man, or whose loud laugh and constant banter are nothing more than a ten-foot pole to prevent others from coming too close to the thin tissue of which the real man feels that he is made?

IV

What are the remedies?

The most fundamental remedy, to repeat, is the conviction of the individual regarding his own personal worth. This is not false pride or snobbery. It should not mean the assumption of powers or talents that one does not possess. Nor should it imply that others are less endowed or worthy than oneself. As a matter of fact, this conviction has no immediate reference to anyone else. It means simply and primarily the realization of one's place in God's creative act and providence. I must remind myself that I am God's image and likeness. To think less of myself than God does, who by His infinite power has created me, is to give small credit to Him. The world has been made for me to work in creatively. Life's fulfillment and life's friendships are to be found in the expression of my own powers and in the faith I have in myself, or they are not to be found at all.

There is ample Christian authority for reliance on these principles. It is true that Christ stressed the necessity of humility and referred to His own heart as "meek and humble."[1] But humility, as a true and broad vision of oneself in the view of God and of one's responsibilities to mankind, must not be confused with self-contempt or abject fear. Christ impressed even the scribes and pharisees as one "having power."[2] He constantly stressed the dignity of the individual in the eyes of God, pointing out that if God thus regards the lilies of the field, "how much more you, O ye of little faith."[3] The serenity and poise of Christ's personality flowed in large part from the perfect awareness of His power and purpose.

This same confidence He imparted to His Apostles. It was only when they lapsed back into their original fears and shiftlessness that they experienced failure. St. Peter, who started to walk upon the water, sank into the waves when faith in himself as well as in Christ began to weaken. St. Paul, who "gloried" in his infirmities, never relinquished the faith in himself which he learned from Christ. This doctrine of self-assurance, which he raises to a supernatural level through the gift of grace, shines through all his epistles. Did not Christ Himself say to His followers: "You are the light of the world. A city seated on a mountain cannot be hid. Neither do men light a candle and put it under a bushel, but upon a candlestick, that it

[1] Matt. 11:29.
[2] Matt. 7:29.
[3] Luke 12:28.

may shine to all that are in the house. So let your light shine before men that they may see your good works and glorify your Father who is in heaven."[4]

The application of this principle must come first of all in a realistic and honest view of one's own powers, neither exaggerating falsely nor, on the other hand, cowardly shrinking from responsibilities. This means I must honestly recognize that I am capable of doing certain things, that these things are definitely useful and worthy, and that I am not to deceive myself by vainly reaching for ambitions that are beyond my powers or outside my talents or to allow myself to become discouraged by the realization that what I might like to do or be may be reserved for others.

Too many people waste their lives in pining for the opportunities of others and in passing by the very real powers and opportunities that they themselves possess. Worse still, this inactivity is often the result of our envy for the imaginary privileges of others. Edward R. Sill reminds us in his striking poem *Opportunity:*

This I beheld, or dreamed it in a dream:
There spread a cloud of dust along a plain;
And underneath the cloud, or in it, raged
A furious battle, and men yelled, and swords
Shocked upon swords and shields. A prince's banner
Wavered, then staggered backward, hemmed by foes.

A craven hung along the battle's edge,
And thought, "Had I sword of keener steel –
That blue blade that the king's son bears – but this
Blunt thing!" – he snapped and flung it from his hand,
And lowering crept away and left the field.

---

[4] Matt. 5:14–16.

Then came the king's son, wounded, sore bestead,
And weaponless, and saw the broken sword,
Hilt-buried in the dry and trodden sand,
And ran and snatched it, and with battle-shout
Lifted afresh he hewed his enemy down,
And saved a great cause that heroic day.

How many glorious achievements have been the result, not of perfect instruments and ideal circumstances, but of confident determination in the use of second-rate implements and frequently in surroundings that might dishearten or deceive a timid soul. The blunt swords that we snap in disgust and leave "hilt-buried in the dry and trodden sand" are the opportunities that we pass by, for others of greater vision than ourselves to seize and make the most of.

How many persons, apparently frustrated in their secret ambition to follow a literary career, remain forever inarticulate, fretting for opportunities and contacts beyond their reach and failing to see the beauty or to recognize the real possibilities of the life around them. Many of the finest gems of literature have been penned by men and women who worked in silence and obscurity, using such humble materials to write upon as the backs of envelopes, as Lincoln is said to have done when writing his immortal Gettysburg Address. How many a youth with artistic ability sinks into despair because of reverses or because of the poor materials at his disposal. Nevertheless, many of the world's greatest masterpieces were painted by poor men with homemade brushes on canvases that had been used before and in attics that knew no comfort beyond that of meager shelter. How much money has been wasted on music lessons for children who despise the routine of scales and drills, or conceal their lack of persistence by complaining of the inferior instruments they are given to use. But many of the most exquisite compositions have been wrought on decidedly cheap instruments. The great Beethoven scorned his own deafness, to write some of his greatest works.

One of the principal causes of a sense of aimlessness in life and of an immense waste of valuable energy consists in a positive evasion of the patient work that is required to develop oneself. As a result, many people never grow up, but remain as pathetic children running from responsibility. Another cause is the failure to appraise the moral values that may underlie the humblest occupations and the simplest existence. In his story, *The Great Stone Face,* Nathaniel Hawthorne has given a beautiful illustration of the manner in which the humble things in life may lead to splendid results, even without our conscious realization of what is happening within us. The story of the boy Ernest, daily studying the great qualities of the face carved by nature on the mountain side and daily striving to make himself worthy of the prophesied day when a stranger would come into the valley bearing its features and reflecting its glory, has a poignant lesson for everyone. For just as Ernest himself proved to be the fulfillment of the prophecy, everyone must find the realization of life in pursuing for himself the possibilities inherent in his own occupations and duties.

Why is it that we should fall back into discouragement with ourselves if no great tests of courage or special opportunities are given us to demonstrate our worth? The secret of discovering our purpose, of developing ourselves to higher possibilities, lies in the unsuspected gold of situations in daily life, in the little opportunities of giving service and of bearing burdens that are so small we hardly think them worth the while. The cheerful mind achieves greatness and universality, precisely because it goes out to identify itself with the constructive purposes of creation and to operate for the benefit of others, no matter how small the community or how limited the sphere of action.

Now is the time to offer to God what we have. Tomorrow may be too late. Now is the time to determine upon the radiation of a helpful influence, going out of our way to make friends, interpreting life genially and sympathetically, making our contribution to it, gladly sharing with others the spark of divine light that is ours to brighten the darkness.

Even in His moment of deepest anguish, Christ confidently prayed forgiveness for His enemies and generously commended His spirit to God, the Father. If He had surrendered to dejection. He would have given up on a thousand scores. But He saw beyond His apparent failure and His crucifixion – and therein lay His final triumph.

Chapter 3

SELF-PERSPECTIVE AND SUCCESS

"Blessed are the meek, for they shall possess the land" (Matt. 5:4).

I

THE Beatitudes of Christ, particularly if they are considered as formulas for happiness and success (and there is no reason why they should not), seem to be the declaration of contraries. General sentiment would never select meekness as a requirement or even as a desirable quality for one who sets out to possess the land – to gain power and exercise a lasting influence on this sphere. On the contrary, self-assurance and aggressiveness are considered essential for success in a world where competition is keen and ruthless.

In establishing an intimate connection between happiness and holiness, however, Christ indicated a much larger program and a different set of values than are generally conceived under the title of possession of the land. Christ had in mind, not so much the acquisition of wealth or temporal advantages, as the possession of those spiritual qualities and powers of appreciation which bring the universe to one's door and make life, as we say, worth living. Wealth, leisure, pleasure, social position, and public power do not by themselves make life worth living. They can exist, and often do, together with useless and extremely unhappy lives.

The popular mind conceives happiness as something to be enjoyed in the manner of a luxury after the struggle. There is, to be sure, an element of the same idea in the Christian promise of eternal joy for a life of virtue. But, strictly speaking, the rewards of Christian service are already in a great measure bound up intimately with the service itself. The second Beatitude is much more than the declaration of a reward for faithful service, like a sweet held out to a child for good behavior. It is a divine assurance that from meekness there flows a continuous strength and development of the soul, bearing its own reward now and proceeding steadily toward an eternal union with God, as from a flower there rises a beauty of color and delicacy of perfume. In a word, Christ pointed out one of the secrets of happiness; and happiness, if we conceive it profoundly, is salvation.

The fulfillment of happy expectations depends largely on the standard of values upon which people build their lives and cast their fate. Personal vision, shaped by birth, education, and environment, plays a large part in determining this standard, independently of the laws of right and wrong; and, as a result, the things in life that are relatively satisfactory for some persons are disgusting or ridiculous in the eyes of others. Devotees of *fast* life, particularly those who throw themselves into sensual pleasures, look with pity and scorn upon others whose vision is pure and exalted. Those whose idea of conviviality centers around irresponsible drinking become thoroughly impatient with the reticence of more temperate persons. At the same time there is an unconscious tendency in most of mankind to create a balance between actions and ideals. A man who does not live as his conscience dictates will find himself gradually beginning to adjust his ideals to fit his way of acting.

The reason why many people find more joy in the anticipation of their desires than in their actual fulfillment is simply that they have been led to adopt a false ideal. Up to the moment of rude awakening they are led on by the illusion of a false hope. Then the crisis arrives, and they suddenly behold the whole structure of their lives crumbling beneath them. The man or the woman who stakes everything on wealth, gratification of passion, artistic ambition, love, political power, can easily come to doubt the value of existence itself when the object of desire eludes the grasp or demonstrates its inability to satisfy. Persons for whom the interest of life has departed may come to feel that there is no comparison between the momentary pangs of a self-inflicted death and the prolonged agonies of a joyless earthly career.

For most of us, the building of a high ideal of life is a long and difficult process. It is not unlike the development of a taste for fine art or music. One whose early appreciation of music has been formed on cheap ballads is likely to find grand opera ridiculous and a Beethoven symphony a tremendous bore. Only by patience and an implicit trust in the guiding judgment of others who understand music can he hope to develop an appreciation of a masterpiece. Then, as he looks back over this process of development, he comes to realize how puny and weak his original outlook really was. For those whose ideal of life is one of artificial excitement and indulgence, the ideal of Christ may require an even more painful readjustment; and those whose standard of life is the satisfaction of every impulse must have the courage to break their spirit before they can build it up along the solid lines of Christian meekness.

This is particularly true of persons who have been able to satisfy every whim and desire. Easy sailing in life, the consciousness of superiority, and the ability to impose one's will upon others can readily produce a selfish egotism and sterility of character. In a way, nature itself contributes toward such development, and its processes have to be corrected and synchronized as time goes on. Infants in swaddling clothes, because they are forced to depend upon their parents in every need, suppress no desires and spare no one the pains of waiting on them. The little attentions, the baby talk, and adulation of adoring relatives only increase the budding idea of children that they must possess something decidedly superior, and this idea has to undergo much painful modification before the youngsters become acceptable to society. The process of teaching little children to respect the right of ownership itself is often so difficult that it can be placed only in terms which often encourage a selfish point of view. Children are often led to think that while they have no right to take the toys of other children or use them without permission, they can do whatever they wish with their own things and even destroy them to keep others from getting pleasure from them.

Everyone recalls the bully of the school yard and

the rule of terror he imposed upon his playmates until someone came along, perhaps a quiet, unimpressive lad, who thrashed him out of his conceit. Every back lot has its petty tyrants, boys and girls who insist on managing all the games, under threat of breaking up the fun or running home with loud cries and torrents of tears to foolish, all-believing mothers. The observation of children at play has much to teach us. We are, all of us, only children, with a few inches added to our height or girth, and a few years of mostly unavailing experience.

Village choirs, parochial dramatic societies, college orchestras, and neighborhood social and cultural leagues, the world over, have the same difficulties; and there is no organization or community so lofty or grand that it can afford to laugh at the little ambitions and jealousies of less pretentious groups, without a pang of mortification for its own. In the national assembly of grand regents as well as in the local reading circle, in the grand opera as well as in the first enterprise of home talent, the same problems appear, of letting conceited persons down gently, of distributing the honors fairly, and of giving people at least the illusion that they are fully appreciated.

Rivals for the tenor and soprano solos must be placated. Aspirants for the rôles of leading man and leading lady have to be coaxed and cajoled, with mingled flattery and apology, before they can be brought into a manageable attitude. Some of the first fiddles are obliged to consider the beauty, the dignity, and the loudly applauded necessity of becoming second fiddles, so the orchestra can produce a harmony. Opponents for the offices of permanent chairman, secretary, and treasurer, must be pacified, if possible, by appointment to specially created positions which have an atmosphere of superlative dignity but in reality carry no responsibility; and their cliques must be gently fanned into seeing the advantages of remaining within the organization.

When all this fails, good, courageous common sense must come to the rescue and purge out all elements that are so self-opinionated that they cannot exist in society except in a leading rôle. Temperament is often expressed in the exacting demands of an artist or capable leader for a high standard of excellence and an insistence upon the proper tools and the right working conditions. But it is just as often only an awkward camouflage for inferior qualifications and a furious ambition.

Persons with talent, real or imaginary, are under a tremendous natural handicap. If it is real and recognized by others, it brings with it the burden of success, which is the subtle, but often overpowering development of what someone has called a "fatty degeneration of the ego." Any achievement that puts one in the public eye also builds up the perfumed fog of flattery, and blessed is he who can penetrate it. On the other hand, those whose craving for recognition far outstrips their real merit and remains largely ungratified take refuge in a little world of self-delusion and an exotic atmosphere, where they can offer incense to themselves and affect a contempt for the world they secretly worship.

Great men, of course, in the democracy of spirit and universal sympathy which makes them great, are seldom given to this gnawing at the heart. Even in the praise laid at their feet, they are ready to recognize the elements of insincerity and snobbishness as distinct from the sincere and considerate tribute. Their sense of humor is always at hand to prevent them from falling backward with conceited gullibility, in moments of applause, or from devouring themselves with self-pity, in moments of loneliness. They are ready to learn wisdom from the pauper as well as from the prince, and to realize that life and inspiration run deepest where the simple, elemental things are foremost and where poverty and suffering are not unknown. It is the little fellow, whose eyes are on the moon and whose heart is in his vest pocket, who swells to the bursting point at the thought of his personal endowments. If he is an artist, he flaunts his frustration in the form of affectation in dress and manner. Eccentric dress, unconventional morality, and incomprehensible art often form the atmospheric compensation for the tremendous gap that lies between the artist's estimate of himself and the ingenuous silence of the public.

As a mark of the truly great, however, humility is a comparatively rare virtue, even among those who arrive at eminence in their field. There is no reason why a person should not aim to improve himself culturally, financially, and socially. But the difficulty of advance is that few people are capable of realizing the extent to which elements outside and previous to themselves have contributed to their success. The millionaire and the socially élite may despise the humble cottage of the poor and the simple joys and faiths of their forefathers. Nevertheless, it is upon this foundation that their own rise has been made possible, and from the rugged strength and solid virtue of these things permanence is given to the social and financial structure upon which they rest so content. It is easy for one who has been hoisted to the pinnacle of worldly fame and prosperity to look down with a contemptuous gaze upon such things as religion, worship, moral safeguards, frugality, and sympathy for the oppressed and for those less fortunate than themselves. With something of this idea, Gray penned his immortal lines in the *Elegy Written in a Country Churchyard,* musing on what might have been, had the simple souls asleep in the grave been afforded an ampler field of action:

> The applause of listening senates to command,
> The threats of pain and ruin to despise,
> To scatter plenty o'er a smiling land,
> And read their history in a nation's eyes,
>
> Their lot forbade: not circumscribed alone
> Their growing virtues, but their crimes confined;
> Forbade to wade through slaughter to a throne,
> And shut the gates of mercy on mankind,
>
> The struggling pangs of conscious truth to hide,
> To quench the blushes of ingenuous shame,
> Or heap the shrine of luxury and pride
> With incense kindled at the Muse's flame.

This curious transformation which Gray suggests is often observable in persons who are placed in positions of authority. As private individuals, they were charming and unaffected; in an official capacity, they become ruthless, overbearing, and intolerable. The consciousness of power works havoc to their humane qualities, perhaps despite themselves. Then their period of office expires. Their charm returns, and they greet their friends and their former subordinates with an easy grace, which, had they possessed it together with authority, would have stamped them as genuine leaders. The same is true of many who have gone through evil days and lost their prosperity and prestige. They return to the God of poverty whom they were unable to recognize as the God of plenty. They begin again the pious exercise of their religious duties, and they are glad to greet old friends whom they could hardly distinguish in the blinding glare of wealth and honor.

II

If we examine pride psychologically, we shall probably discover that its causes and effects upon its victims are pretty much alike. In nearly every case, the afflicted individual comes into the possession or the fancied possession of some power, knowledge, ability, or material advantage. He believes that this acquisition is due principally to his own genius and that it is a proof of his own superiority. As a result, he concludes that there is no longer use in consulting others for advice, since they are hopelessly antiquated or unable to grasp his vision; and he refuses to risk the possible humiliation of contradiction by entering into a discussion of his plans. People infected with pride are poor losers, because the very assumption of defeat completely demolishes their whole mental fabric.

Young students, whose eyes are beginning to open to the secrets of life, come to the easy conclusion that the advice and suggestions of their parents with regard to persons and places is absurd. They cannot conceive the possibility of older persons' being acquainted with the problems of youth. They are intolerant of a conservative outlook. They dismiss the past as "medieval" and fabulous. The pride of life, which is the impulsive.

unreflecting urge of natural forces in their veins, makes them restive under restraint and intolerant of contradiction. Then come a series of disasters, disillusions, tragedy in love, betrayals of confidence; and they enter mature life often with a cynical outlook and a sour self-sufficiency – unless they have learned to compare notes with others and submit their judgment to that of older and more experienced persons.

A similar process often takes place in men of ambition who are unable to accept criticism or suggestions from others. Once in power, they shelve others of mature wisdom, and they surround themselves with straw men who are capable only of nodding assent to every word of the master or are crafty enough to realize that a dissenting opinion would spell disaster to their own careers. It is seldom upon this basis that mankind has received permanent benefit.

Professional men, doctors, lawyers, and even the clergy, are especially subject to an egotistical formation; and the deeper that one goes in the hierarchy of careers and professions, the more arrogant and unyielding the professional manner may become. Anyone whose knowledge and training are denied to the general public and who, on the other hand, enjoys the humble confidences of the public in a professional or official capacity has a tendency to enthrone himself behind an increasingly impersonal attitude toward the world and the people in it. Those who are particularly shallow in spirit find no trouble in believing that the public seeks them out, not because of their technical skill, which has been handed them in school or granted them by opportunities for experience, but because of some inherent superiority or divinity of their own.

The first temptation the young clergyman, fresh from the seminary, has to face is that of the doffing of hats and the deference shown him by men who are his superiors in years, experience, wisdom, and perhaps in character. If he is more susceptible to flattery than is safe for one of the cloth, he may even come under the secret and ridiculous illusion that the attentions of the flock are due to the dash and charm of his personality, when he might not provoke even a passing glance, were he divested of his official character. Doctors and lawyers can become extremely overbearing and nasty toward their office help and assistants, and in their homes they may adopt a stern paternalism and air of superiority toward their wives. Many a wife of a professional man finds herself a kind of creature tolerated in the establishment of her husband. Domestic problems in such a case are not solved by mutual discussion. She finds that she must consult her husband at the proper hours and carry out his orders with the obedience of an invalid on a diet and on a regime of bitter pills or of a client whose position is very weak and can be maintained only by exact obedience to her legal adviser.

III

Conceited pride has a twofold weakening effect, one of walling up its victim from realities, and the other of making him supersensitive to anything that might be construed to indicate a belittling attitude on the part of others. Both effects, of course, are intimately connected. Football teams, prize fighters, opera singers, gamblers, speculators in stocks and bonds, drivers of automobiles, politicians, businessmen, authors, and living saints are all alike in this: that they are at their very weakest and are most ripe for a fall at the moment of supremest confidence. The turkey that struts in the barnyard is never so engrossed in his plumage and so little apprehensive of the future as during the fat weeks preceding Thanksgiving Day.

The situation may be reversed, and it is equally true that no man has struck the bottom of destiny until his pride has pinned him down from seeking the mercy and aid of his friends. When a man becomes secretive, hiding himself away from his friends, his end has come. He may sink ever so low, but if he can bring himself to the point of facing his loyal associates and his family and of accepting the stern truth from their lips, there is still hope of redemption. What is true in the social order is true also in the spiritual order. Despair of God's mercy is often no more than a tremendous self-pity and an unconquerable pride that insists on glorifying its own sense of shame to such titanic proportions that it seems to dwarf even the power of God. The same is often true of scrupulous persons who are unable to settle their moral doubts and fears. Cast into the extremities of self-distrust, they still refuse to submit their judgment to that of a spiritual adviser, and they may even come to enjoy secretly the morose luxury of mental confusion.

The personal sensitiveness which frequently accompanies these mental states also arrives at ridiculous proportions. Sensitiveness amounting to ready resentment of every word of criticism or indication of belittlement may be a constitutional handicap accompanying a high-strung nervous system. At times it may be a by-product of the widely publicized "inferiority complex," struggling to break through a natural bashfulness or trying to ward off what it feels is a patronizing attitude on the part of others. Some persons labor heavily under the illusion that their associates look down upon them, and that every humorous remark and bit of chaff is intended as a shaft of ridicule to put them in their place; and it is only in the gradual realization that they are quite as good as the rest of the crowd and able to exchange with experiences on an equal basis, that they lose their bitter secret pride and come out into the open air of naturalness and charm.

This extreme sensitiveness shows itself most obviously among little children. A quick word, even a stern glance, is often enough to send them into torrents of tears. Some people begin life with a chip on their shoulders and go through life hoping and praying that someone will come along to knock it off and give them a chance to display their resentment. They take offense over every trifle. They see an insult in every remark. They demand a formal apology for every slight. They are unwilling to yield, themselves; and sooner than come to a compromise, they are prepared to lose the friends of a lifetime over incidents that could be dismissed with a laugh or a simple regret. When difficulties arise, they immediately assume that everyone else is wrong; and it would be impossible for them, for the sake of peace, to take even partial blame for any mishap that might arise.

Every office force has at least one individual who feels that the world is down on him, that he is passed over for men of lesser ability, that his merits are unrecognized; and when the moment for promotion comes, he is unprepared for it, because he feels that he is only second or third choice and that someone must have refused it before him. There are comparatively few women who can be relied upon to substitute at a bridge party for an invited guest who has been unable to come, particularly if they think they should have been invited in the first place. In general, it may be said that we are all inclined to be sulky when asked to do favors for which little recognition or honor is accorded, and even in the favors extended us we are often inclined to suspect that perhaps we are only a second choice.

Persons in public life particularly are called upon to face the problem of oversensitive persons. Teachers have to be constantly on their guard against saying or doing things that would give the pupils any justification for complaining to overcredulous parents and bringing down parental wrath upon their own heads. Officials who have offices to distribute or privileges to extend soon find themselves surrounded by menacing friends and angry supplicants who are ready to cry injustice, favoritism, and incompetence unless their every whim is justified. Taxpayers who are loudest in their complaints against increased and multiplied assessments are often the most disgruntled if the governmental pay rolls are reduced and they or their friends and relations are eliminated in the process. Then begins a whispering campaign against officialdom.

In church affairs, where one might expect people to exercise the greatest patience and good will, the mightiest tempests arise, often over affairs which are quite trivial in themselves. The clergyman overlooks someone at the communion rail, and immediately he is denounced by the person whose sensibilities he has unwittingly wounded. If someone's little girl does not lead her class, it is because of unfair discrimination on his part and utter incompetence on the part of the teachers in his school. If he has wealthy friends, it is because he caters to the rich. If he visits the poor, it is to gain publicity for himself. A little tiff over the pew rent, a slight rebuke for arriving late at church services, and some people become implacable bolshevists against all religious affiliations.

There is nothing so effective in checking the ingrowing pains of pride as a sense of humor or a sense of perspective, which is, perhaps, one of the first requisites for humor. People who take themselves too seriously need the antidote of a good laugh to reduce values to their true level and to declare a permanent moratorium on many of their pet grievances and frustrated ambitions. Nursing ancient hates, maintaining a hostile silence for those who have wounded our pride, and keeping up an artificial illusion of personal rights and qualifications which sincerely we know do not exist, is like retaining old magazines and pieces of bric-a-brac, in the vain hope that they may come to be of use. From time to time a courageous sweeping out and burning of the accumulation is necessary to prevent the breeding of disease germs and to make room for worthwhile things.

The battle against pride in no way implies the loss of self-respect or self-confidence. On the contrary, it means the elimination of such excess mental baggage as obstructs a general view of ourselves and hinders progress. No one is so mentally muscular and fit for life as he who realizes his limitations and is prepared to make a genuine struggle for the ideal which lies far beyond him. No one has greater self-respect than he who refuses to believe that he has reached the height of his powers or that he is so fortified that he is incapable of making the same mistakes and falling into the same traps as others. Self-confidence does not mean a belligerent attitude toward life or a desire to fight and prove which is the better man on every occasion. Permanent peace and true progress have been built, not upon a leap to arms, but upon that quiet restraint, forbearance, and further study which humility and meekness counsel.

The Holy Scriptures verify all that common sense can say on this subject. The angels and Adam and Eve fell through pride. David was punished for his pride; and when Christ wished to point out the weakness of the Jews and their leaders, He could find no more expressive word than "stiff-necked." His own life was filled, not only with the preaching of humility, but with its practice. He was able to say, without fear of contradiction, "Learn of me, for I am meek and humble of heart."[1] Possession of the land, possession of life in its fullest and most progressive sense, the appreciation of values that lead to eternal happiness, beginning with this life, can come only from humility. In her canticle of praise, the Blessed Virgin Mary uttered a truth that has the force of a universal divine law: "He hath put down the mighty from their seats, and hath exalted the humble."[2] There is no greater mistake than to suppose that one is too good for the work he is called upon to do. The secret of success consists in doing well and proudly the work at hand, no matter how humble it may seem.

---

[1] Matt. 11:29.
[2] Luke 1:52.

CHAPTER 4

SELF-DISCIPLINE AND HAPPINESS

"For the beginning of [Wisdom] is the most true desire of discipline. And the care of discipline is love: and love is the keeping of her laws" (Wisdom 6:18, 19).

I

THE greatest heresy of our age is undoubtedly that which asserts that happiness arises spontaneously and exclusively from complete freedom. Freedom is thus understood as the absence of personal restraints, conventions, or "taboos," and the ability to indulge oneself and one's desires and appetites without asking the thousand and one questions that seem to make up the fabric of social and personal morality. It may be that the realization of such an ideal is quite beyond the range of possibility. Nevertheless, very many persons have decided for themselves that they can be happy only when they can have all the things they desire and do all the things they wish.

In a certain sense, this philosophy of happiness is universal, beginning with childhood. Children are unable to understand why they cannot have everything their little hearts desire, why they must eat certain things besides candy, or go to school, or go to bed at certain hours. They crave the time to come when they will be free to do just what they like—as if such a time were ever to come. And it is amazing how the child-mind will build up for itself an excellent line of reasoning for the objects of desire.

In this connection, I recall that, when I was in one of the first grades of school, a clever salesman one day came to our class demonstrating a gadget, which, when attached to a pencil, could be used for transferring graphic material, such as pictures, from the printed page to one's own paper. At noontime, I represented to my parents the urgency of my securing one of these attachments; and, when they hesitated, I actually believed that they were standing in the way of an artistic career. A great deal of persuasion on my part, with tears of mingled resentment and angry frustration, finally broke down their resistance. I bought the article in the conviction that it was essential to my happiness. A few days later I discovered that I had no real use for it. Similar experiences are often repeated throughout the lives of most of us.

In many ways, this impatience to gratify ourselves and dependence upon things outside of ourselves are enlarged by the spirit of the society in which we live, a spirit which we sometimes mistakenly glorify as "the American Way." The ease of self-indulgence in the United States is truly remarkable. Modern inventions and conveniences have become a passion with us and have so dominated our lives that it is practically impossible, particularly in urban communities, for people to do for themselves the things that made up much of the activity of the pioneers. Our high standard of living has all but eliminated the little domestic chores that children were once called upon to do, so that the offspring of the poor usually have as much time on their hands as those of the rich.

As a result, a great many children are today growing up incapable of doing the most elemental things for themselves or of undertaking tasks that require a sense of responsibility. In part, this difficulty may be due to the aimlessness of much contemporary education. But the fact is that, side by side with the amazing opportunities and advantages of the American people, there is a widespread lack of personal objective and initiative, and increased desire to avoid work or to do the minimum, and a hesitancy to undertake anything that may mean self-denial, self-discipline, and self-sacrifice. This is so evident that a great many observers of the scene have long been in favor of compulsory military training for our young men as a means, quite apart from national defense, of instilling moral stamina into our youth, a task in which our public educational system appears to have failed. Something similar might also be devised, at least in purpose, for the girls of the nation, if selfishness and evasion of social responsibility are not to spoil the world in which we live.

Of course, much depends upon our definitions. But if we define happiness as activity conformable to right order or the fulfillment of desire in accordance with our general good, we are immediately confronted with the problem of self-discipline. Self-discipline means governing oneself and one's appetites according to good reason and judgment, and it applies both to persons and to things.

I am not now referring to *self-denial,* which is far more limited than self-discipline. The former means curtailing or eliminating certain forms of pleasure or gratification, simply as an exercise of the will or as an act for some spiritual objective, let us say as a proof of love or trustworthiness. There is no merit in self-denial apart from the motive or purpose for which it is practised. Whether I eat a dish of ice cream or not, for example, is in itself of no consequence, and acquires spiritual significance only when the decision involves something like saving the money for a worthier cause or letting someone else enjoy the dish or foregoing the enjoyment as an act of love, however small the effort, for God. Self-discipline, however, has a definite value in itself, inasmuch as it enters into the very character of the act itself, examining its value, at times in terms of the moral law and always in terms of common sense and right measure.

Emphasis must be placed on *self*-discipline, for it is only on this basis that a person can live maturely and creatively. External guidance and correctives are generally necessary for the formation of character and the development of sane attitudes and habits; but unless this discipline, imposed from the outside, becomes assimilated by the individual for his own guidance and personal responsibility, its value is very small. I recall that an academy which I once attended forbade the smoking of cigarettes to all the students. On the trains going home for the holidays, however, the boys frequently made up for lost time by smoking five to ten cigarettes at the same time and arrived at their destinations in a collapsed condition. Evidently the rule failed in its purpose of character formation.

Unless external discipline is accompanied by rational explanation or is obviously reasonable, it can generate a rebellious spirit. Discipline in the home which goes so far as to tyrannize over the children often begets a spirit of deceit and dissipation. The same has been true of a good deal of the old academic discipline, including that of certain Catholic schools, which sometimes failed, in their rigor, to give youth an opportunity of testing itself under direction, and succeeded only in producing an unconvinced mentality and rather bewildered attitude toward life. An appeal to the "will of God" as the all satisfying motive for obeying regulations can oversimplify the problem of discipline, and, unless joined with habits of personal responsibility and self-respect, can end in creating hollow and superficial virtue.

Self-discipline is essentially a matter of *will* power or of habits developed through repeated voluntary acts, but it must begin with certain fundamental attitudes of the mind. The mind itself must be disciplined to accept certain absolute values, particularly in the moral order, and to apply these standards as tests in selecting practical alternatives of action. Unless one starts out with at least some convictions which will stand up in a crisis, it is impossible to speak of self-discipline. An unprincipled person can always find a good reason for any type of conduct and can "rationalize" the acceptance of any situation.

I can remember my father's frequent reference to people as divided into two classes, those of principled personality or character and those of unprincipled outlook. As a child, I wondered just what this meant; but I realize now what he had in mind. The principled man can be depended on to act upon a given code of right and wrong according to his lights. The unprincipled person is essentially unreliable and unpredictable, since for him "anything goes," depending on the whim of the moment and the appeal of momentary satisfaction or advantage.

Lack of principle is not to be confused with impulsiveness, which is decision without sufficient reflection. Nevertheless, judged by their results, the two faults are frequently alike. Mental discipline requires more than instincts of the right, the good, and the appropriate; it must include also a certain calm and reasoning spirit before coming to a conclusion or launching on a course of action. For that matter, it means also a willingness to abide by tested principles and sound teaching. The notion that a person must himself test and taste every experience to discover the truth is quite false and can become exceedingly harmful. Personal experience is not required for wisdom, as many a tragedy can bear witness.

Closely allied with the spirit of reflection is the practice of repose and mental relaxation. To a certain extent, the activity of the mind is a reflection of one's physical condition, and vice versa. High-strung persons and those with much nervous energy are likely to have overactive minds. Nevertheless, this energy can be brought under control, partly by the determination to rid the mind of much rubbish and wasted activity and partly by establishing physical controls. No one should allow himself to become excessively tired, if he can prevent it. This means that at regular intervals during the day, the eyes should be closed for a few minutes, or one should take out a little time in which to relax. At such intervals the mind should be cleared, either by dampening all mental activity or, by broadening mental activity in striving for spiritual union with the mind of God.

II

To a large extent, the activity of the mind, although a spiritual operation of the soul, is affected by that of the imagination, which is an organic faculty of the material brain and nervous system. Because the entire physical system is closely linked together, it is only natural that various elements within the body should affect the condition and operation of the imagination. It is for this reason that excessive fatigue can distort the pictures projected in the brain and lead to abnormal mental activity. A run-down physical condition will also impair healthy thought and render mental discipline difficult. Lack of proper exercise, excessive indulgence in food as well as in drink, and faulty metabolism can give rise to various disturbances of the imagination. Organic defects or special conditions reflect themselves definitely in mental states, so much so that a surgical operation or particular medical care may be required to relieve physical pressure causing worried or excited states of mind and fantastic conditions of the imagination.

Persons who are excessively fatigued are likely to make decisions quite unrepresentative of their normal outlook. Sick persons and the aged frequently develop suspicious attitudes and persecution complexes with no other foundation than that of impaired physical faculties. Some of the most pious persons in the world are tormented by bitter feelings and fantastically immoral thoughts, simply as the result of a bodily condition or organic derangements. Abnormal sexual suggestions and mental pictures, irritability, and dejection may well be examined in the light of these considerations.

Prayer alone is not usually sufficient to drive away foul thoughts, nor can pious ejaculations solve the complete problem of a brooding mind. Discipline of the imagination means that some attention must be given to healthy, well-rounded living. Fresh air, healthy, moderate eating, proper exercise, and plenty of rest are almost as much a part of mental discipline as are logic and ontology, and certainly must supplement spiritual activity.

At the same time, direct action has to be taken in the management of the imagination itself. The imagination, together with the nervous system, is like a garden. It must be carefully planted, carefully weeded, and kept in right order, if it is to serve a constructive purpose. The senses themselves must be disciplined, if mental calm and mastery are to be preserved. In a word, an orderly and controlled intellectual life means a definite "no" to a great many things.

It is impossible to keep a clean mind, no matter how physically fit a person may be, if he allows himself to view lewd spectacles, or to read suggestive literature and indulge in filthy conversation. The effect of such activity is not only to stimulate the nervous system to immediate excitement, but also to store up certain reflexes which recur at apparently unrelated times and in a way that is largely beyond control. Clean thinking and calm, objective attitudes are developed, not suddenly, but through long, careful practice and determined vigilance.

The same is true of an even disposition. There are

certain topics that arouse nearly everyone to anger or to bitter excitement. One must learn to avoid discussing them. Persons with a strong temper must make a special effort to swallow their pride and forego the expression of their convictions when they feel their psychological heat rising. It is true that certain individuals are temperamentally inclined to "fly off the handle." Possibly, this may be excused in children, but there is no reason for it in adults, who have had plenty of time to learn and practise the art of self-discipline. The unpleasant spectacle of a grown person's screaming with rage may arouse our pity, but it is a pity tempered with contempt.

In most instances, the reason for an unmanageable imagination and for nervous hysteria is to be found, at least partially, in the failure to develop positive outlooks through creative mental activity and intellectual interests. A person who is interested in the world of affairs, of books, of hobbies, and above all in his own work, is not likely to become the prey of every passing fancy, worry, or phantasm. A person with a well-stocked mind will not find it difficult to drive out mental weeds and cockles.

The development of intellectual interests, of course, can hardly serve a constructive purpose if it is merely an escape, even from noxious mental and imaginative activity. There should always be some positive objective in view, some idea of making oneself more useful to society, some broadening and deepening of one's understanding and sympathies, some expression of one's creative talents. For this reason, the careful selection of a hobby, whether it be stamp collecting, music, art, or any one of a thousand activities that mean systematic and progressive mental development, is a wise and fruitful form of self-discipline.

Persons who can co-ordinate their activities in line with their special work, and take their supreme interest and pleasure in their work, have learned the inner secret of this development. The housewife whose interests are co-ordinated into making her home and family as ideal as possible, the nurse who perfects herself to be of service to the sick, the merchant, doctor, lawyer, clergyman, farmer, or factory hand who wishes to do his work supremely well and who develops his mind and imagination in line with his avocation is bound to achieve success in ever widening circles and to live life, not in a desultory fashion, but according to a plan. The unhappiest of all people are those for whom life begins only after working hours.

It may not be amiss to repeat the advisability of a careful selection of material for thought. Every mind is impressionable, and the influence, for example, of what we read is far greater than most people recognize. In this connection, I may mention the case of a young woman who asked my advice with respect to her loss of faith in God and in religion. She assured me that she had, in the spirit of inquiry, delved into the works of such writers as Nietzsche, Schopenhauer, and Anatole France, but that none of these books had any effect upon her independent thinking. Incidentally, she was now on the point of marrying a boy who entertained the same views about life as herself. But when I suggested that she read one or two books that I mentioned as a corrective to her previous mental fare, she hastily declined, on the grounds that such reading might upset her mental equilibrium. Insincerity and mental discipline are incompatible with each other.

Naturally, any program of mental development and control means a disciplining of energies. For over-ambitious persons, such discipline will take the form of husbanding their resources and making a proper selection between activities according to their values. Persons of talent frequently dissipate their energies by engaging in too many and too variegated enterprises. One cannot hope to do everything and achieve anything well. One of my own ambitions has been to paint; but I have never had the time to follow up this desire, and I think I have done wisely to shelve it. A person leading a busy life must learn to refuse numerous invitations to social affairs, to miss interesting plays, and to admit that he has not read certain "best sellers." Unwise and excessive expenditure of energy can lead only to inferior work and nervous exhaustion.

The more common difficulty, however, is of an opposite sort. The failure of most people to achieve results according to their capacities is due not so much to the reckless expenditure of energies as to the failure to arouse them to proper action. Sloth, it may be recalled, is one of the capital vices and shows itself in every department of personality. There is such a thing as mental laziness. Many persons of extraordinary talent are too lazy to produce anything worth while. It frequently happens, as in the story of the turtle and the hare, that persons of moderate ability, through sheer, plodding determination, outstrip their more clever associates who allow themselves to lapse into a dream world. Slovenly homes, careless personal appearance, and mediocre work are slight indications of what results from sloth. In the last analysis, it may be found that the great catastrophes of the world have been due to sins of omission more than to sins of commission. The individual who is striving for the development of his personality must begin by examining himself on this fundamental point.

III

From the discipline of the mind naturally proceeds the mastery of the other human faculties, notably of the appetites. By the appetites, I mean all the senses and faculties that are capable of pleasurable gratification. Man is half animal, guided and checked in part by his animal instincts; but because he also has a spiritual nature and a free will striving for complete happiness for itself, independently of the corporal function that can be served by sensitive satisfaction, he is capable of voluntary excesses and of the abuse of his bodily faculties. A disciplined mind is essential, therefore, in the right use of the physical appetites, first, to establish right principles and attitudes and, secondly, to allow the pause or reflection necessary to give the will an opportunity to assert itself before the appetites can leap into self-indulgence. In a word, unless reason and the rule of right measure are applied to the senses and to the sensual faculties, a person can become the slave of his body and a victim of his passions.

Herein we must make the vital decision in a philosophy of life. There are those who believe that no repression whatsoever should be put upon the senses and that the only happiness we are sure of is the indulgence of momentary pleasure. As the ancients put it, "Let us eat and drink and make merry today, for tomorrow we die." Others are less philosophical in such a materialistic attitude toward life; but, whether from a pampered childhood or lack of subsequent training or partly from physical weakness, they fail to curb their desires or to practise any form of self-denial. Both types are essentially selfish. The more imperious and demanding they become that others should fit into their scheme of things and serve their whims, the more they exhibit that lack of self-mastery that distinguishes man from the irrational animal.

One of the most widespread current problems in this respect is that of excessive drinking, on the part of both men and women. Refusal to curb this appetite has been responsible for the brutalizing of primitive peoples and for the development of congenital insanity. Precisely the same results can come from intemperance among more highly cultured groups. Among Americans of the middle and upper classes, lack of self-discipline in this matter is frequently indicative of more fundamental, if hidden, forms of instability.

In some cases, recklessness with drink means a lack of internal security and a desire to conceal one's cultural shallowness and lack of human resources by affecting an external bravado. To the extent that drink takes the place of intelligent social intercourse and rational exchange, we may read a serious indictment of the inadequacy of contemporary education. When the normal form of entertainment among people of some pretensions becomes hardly more than maudlin drinking bouts, under whatever name, it is time for the thinking elements of society to utter a profound protest and word of warning. For some people, undisciplined drinking is simply a form of evasion and solace. The maladjusted individual who lacks the courage to study his or her problems honestly and to face life squarely can find an easy escape in a muddled brain.

Not to assume a fanatical or bigoted attitude in this, we are quite safe in laying down the rule that persons who cannot approach drink without excess should leave it alone entirely. For the rest, it should be regarded with care and moderation. Many an excellent career has been ruined by incautious habits of drinking; and a great deal of social life today is being marred by an immature persuasion that a "good time" requires drink in abundance.

In the question of the sexual appetites, we are facing a matter of even graver importance to the individual and to society. In this sphere particularly, self-discipline must be grounded in a sense of moral responsibility. Within recent years, there has been an increasing frankness in sexual education and in the emphasis and even exploitation of sex as a determinant of action. The school of Freudian psychology has regarded sex as the basis of every human phenomenon. Unfortunately, there has not been a corresponding insistence upon moral principles and personal controls to keep the pleasurable phases of this instinct in line with the natural purposes of the sexual faculties. The tendency of pagan sophistication is to extract pleasure from an act and to reject responsibility, thus perverting the very nature of things. Persons who are less extreme in materialistic outlook take refuge in alleging good motives for whatever line of action they choose to adopt.

Such reasoning leads to the disintegration of the individual, of the family, and indeed of society as a whole. To speak of the necessity of law and order in the state and to insist rigorously upon the observance of social usages, while simply ignoring the idea of self-discipline in accordance with predetermined moral law in sexual relations, is absurd in the extreme. The commandment of clean living becomes increasingly difficult as the barriers are thrown down; but in the same measure as irresponsible indulgence comes to prevail, no matter how it is rationalized and glorified, the controls that make for secure and happy living, in accordance with the plan of nature, become endangered.

In a larger sense, the problem of sexual discipline is not a distinct one but is genuinely related with the discipline of all social relationships. The mark of cultural superiority and self-mastery is restraint under all circumstances. Sex is only one of many elements that attract man and woman and hold husband and wife together. As a matter of fact, many strongly sexed individuals are incapable of sustaining social relationships for the reason that they have never learned the meaning of patience, forbearance, and unselfishness. Frequent divorces among many of the most attractive personalities of stage and screen are proof of this. Thousands of unhappy and broken homes, with estranged husbands and wives, and quarreling brothers and sisters, can blame their general failure to control themselves and their unruly desires, for the unhappy condition in which they find themselves.

Underneath all excesses there is, of course, a passionate seeking for happiness. But the principle to be affirmed over and over again is that happiness comes from saying "no" quite as often as from saying "yes," and often from denying oneself the very object that seems most attractive. In companionship, for example, one must learn that there are certain persons and types to be avoided, no matter how lonesome one may be or how powerful the appeal. If we could study this lesson and learn to take counsel from persons of mature judgment, a great deal of unhappiness could be avoided. One of the saddest of my experiences has been that of trying to urge prudence upon young men and women who have become entangled in unfortunate love affairs. With a little caution in the beginning, they might have been spared a great deal of anguish and probably have spared others the same. When involvement reaches a certain stage, it is practically useless to speak of self-discipline or to ask people to turn back.

We are all victimized, not only by the highly nervous age in which we live, but also by the examples we see around us. There is a constant demand for the exciting and the artificial, a dread of dullness and a craving for new experiences. In the face of this pressure, which is frequently part of a gigantic campaign for commercial purposes, it may be necessary for us to pause and take stock of the real nature of things and even to revise our ideas of happiness. We must remind ourselves, from time to time, that we cannot have everything or be everything. There are limits. One cannot play two games at once, or burn the candle at both ends, or, as the saying goes, "have our cake and eat it." Happiness is achieved, not through self-indulgence, but at great cost, in trimming the limits of desire in accordance with the requirements imposed by our respective states of life, by consideration for the social order, and by the moral law.

When we study the life of Christ, our Teacher,

we learn that the secret of the abundant life is to be found in the practice of self-discipline and rational self-denial, not in grasping at every elusive pleasure that shows itself. Infinite Wisdom, Christ, chose the rôle of humility. Infinite Riches, He chose a life of poverty. Infinite Glory, He scorned all earthly honors. Infinite Power, He chose to live with the weak and lowly; and for our sins of overindulgence, our greedy, grasping spirit, and lack of self-control, He permitted Himself to be scourged at the pillar, to be spat upon, to be crowned with thorns, to be hooted at, to be given vinegar and gall to drink, and to die upon the cross.

In accord with that lesson, it must be our endeavor to broaden our conceptions of life's fulfillment upon an unselfish and spiritual basis. The development of Christian personality has to be carried on with the realization that physical pleasure burns itself out in disillusionment and waste unless it is in harmony with the moral law. Character education is essentially a disciplining of the mind and of the human faculties under the determination of the will. There are no short cuts. Good habits are not formed in a single day; but the gradual nature of the process is indicative of the unbounded capacities of the soul growing in the presence of God and sharing in His infinite beatitude.

Chapter 5

CLEAN LIVING AND STABILITY

"O how beautiful is the chaste generation with glory, for the memory thereof is immortal: because it is known both with God and with men" (Wisdom 4:1).

I

THE art of developing a Christian personality is a composite art and study. It embraces a right outlook on life, sound and tested principles of action, personal habits in conformity with law, and self-discipline of appetites. These requirements are nowhere more true and urgent than in that aspect of personality denominated sex. To the extent that a person has mastered the problems arising from sex and turned the impulses of the flesh into strong and generous well-springs of sympathy and lofty action, he has learned the mastery of life itself. In reverse, warped and confused mentality on the subject can beget habits and attitudes far beyond the immediate range of sexual activity and can manifest itself in various forms of personal maladjustment and mischief.

Two general extremes can be held responsible for many of the personal difficulties in the field of character. One, I may refer to as the Puritanical approach;

and the other, as the Libertine approach. In its own way, each is wrong. Each is something of a natural temptation, and the task of achieving a rational equilibrium may call for prolonged and strenuous effort.

The Puritanical approach arises in part from the secret and mysterious aspects of sex and in part to the related elements of human nature itself. Perhaps it can be summed up in the stork story explanation of the origin of human life. Our first introduction to the mystery of life is frequently the idea that children are brought to one's doorstep by that rare bird, the stork, or that they are delivered in the small black valise of a strange man known as the doctor. Parents are usually noncommunicative on this matter, so that boys and girls are initiated into knowledge by their more mature and highly-strung companions, by the prurient jargon that is spawned from private places out into the open on sidewalks and fences, from the occasional revelations of inconsiderate adults, or from sly reading in encyclopedias or family medical books.

The first movements of physical adolescence frequently lead to experimentation with self. Secrecy develops vicious habits. Alley education increases the sense of confusion and shame, and official silence begets the idea that it is better to work out one's salvation in the turmoil of one's own mind. Contact with the outlooks and conduct of others simply heightens the sense of personal confusion and in the entire matter, the adolescent often feels desperately alone.

Very often the growing boy or girl is exposed to a type of squeamish education that makes the problem of comprehension and adjustment still more difficult. Everything is explained in terms of *sin,* and delicacy is pushed so far as to render everything connected with the problems of sex "taboo" and immoral. Without in the least wishing to cast aspersion on the high and noble standards of living taught by the religious orders of men and women and by the clergy, one may note that occasionally overzealous and poorly informed individuals actually succeed in creating false and scrupulous consciences and no end of mental confusion, by imparting an unearthly and quite unrealistic view of sex and of the entire matter of human love. Under the influence of such ideas a girl may mistakenly flee in horror from the very idea of courtship and marriage, and through false motives deprive herself of the legitimate joys of a home and children. Boys and girls alike, unless educated sympathetically in the meaning of their relationships and given a reasonable opportunity to come to know one another as human beings with common problems, can develop strangely warped mentalities or rebel violently against unfair and indeed un-Christian repression.

Years ago many convent schools shuddered at the very thought of any form of social intercourse among boys and girls. Most Catholic boys' schools kept the lads away from the siren lure of young women. Possibly the pendulum in education has now swung too far the other way; but certainly the approach to life cannot be made on a satisfactory basis simply by drawing up a long series of "thou shalt nots" and trusting that well-formed and mature minds and habits will arise spontaneously from a long program of silence, disapproval, prohibition, and chilly condemnation. It has always seemed strange to me that a prayerful people who are taught by the Church to bless "the fruit of thy womb, Jesus," and this from their earliest childhood, should think it unclean and immoral for youth to have a true and adequate idea of what the expression means.

Why this entire outlook of evasion and prudery should exist is difficult to understand. No doubt there is a useful purpose behind the secrecy with which nature itself tends to shroud the more essential and distinctive phases of sexual life. On the other hand, all nature gives ample and open evidence of God's plan, and indeed in terms so simple that a child can grasp it. No one seems to think that there is anything impure in the growth of a plant from a seed. The process of development from flower to fruit is one of the most beautiful phenomena in the world, and a simple explanation of the meaning of pollenization is not likely to give rise to "bad" thoughts. In the same way, the idea of the propagation of animals is quite familiar, and it is seldom that children are shocked even by such intimate scenes as the suckling of pet puppies and kittens. Nearly every child learns that eggs are laid by hens and that baby chicks come from eggs.

There is no reason in the world why the meaning of parenthood, gradually unfolded according to the capacity of the growing mind, should not be one of the most beautiful lessons of youth. There is no reason in the world why considerate parents should not provide a true and adequate explanation of sexual development within the individual, of sexual hygiene, and of rational, Christian methods of meeting the problems and temptations of sexual indulgence as they arise. If in addition to a native personal reticence on the matter children are taught, either directly or by whispered inference, to regard this whole department of their lives and bodies with shame, it is too much to expect them to bare their souls even when they desperately need advice and encouragement. To a certain extent the Confessional can help, but frequently this help is of a sketchy character and comes too late. To serve a genuinely constructive purpose, even the Confessional should find the penitent well instructed in the meaning of sexual processes as well as in the general norms of Christian behavior.

The other extreme, the Libertine approach, is, of course, more rapidly destructive of personal character and of social stability than its opposite. In its basest form, this approach disregards all law and sense of moral responsibility. Sexual indulgence is regarded without further qualification as a normal and free expression of personality — one of life's experiences, with no other guide than that of impulse and no other check than that of social vigilance and respectability. Born of a completely pagan outlook, this philosophy of sex looks only to the gratification of an appetite, detaching so far as possible the element of sensual pleasure from the emotional as well as the physiological purpose of the act. Thus, women are regarded as the legitimate prey of men, and men are regarded simply as brutes for the satisfaction of women. This may perhaps be a crude way of stating the case, but it is substantially the view of persons who have thrown over the Christion conception of love and of the division of the sexes.

In this level of expression, one finds the "dirty" story as a conversation piece, with its lubricious and cynical quip on the physiological aspects of sex life which are rightfully reserved for privacy or with a snigger calling into question the reality of moral standards and endeavors. In the same category comes the perennial crop of "art" in magazine illustrations, in reading matter, in stage and motion picture production, of a nature calculated to stimulate erotic pleasure and nothing more. Not to pause over the fatalistic philosophy which regards the brothel as a necessary concomitant of society, as a sort of slaughterhouse of love, as someone has remarked, this entire school of development finds its logical expression in the casual, if impetuous, demand on the part of men for immediate sexual gratification, in one degree or the other, with women who meet their fancy, and, on the part of women, a kind of expectancy that normal men will invariably reveal the brute in them, given the opportunity.

Thus the graciousness and deep qualities of womanhood are spurned or become the last things realized by the shallow souls for whom only a sudden impulse of flesh means love. Thus the prude and libertine meet on common ground in that neither appreciates the emotional significance of love or the relationship of its physical with its spiritual values. The one flees with horror from what he cannot understand; the other leaps into the burning fire like a fool. For such, the words of Elizabeth Barrett Browning must have an alien sound:

> How do I love thee? Let me count the ways.
> I love thee to the depth and breadth and height
> My soul can reach, when feeling out of sight
> For the ends of Being and ideal Grace.
> I love thee to the level of every day's
> Most quiet need, by sun and candle-light.
> I love thee freely, as men strive for Right;
> I love thee purely, as they turn from Praise.

I love thee with the passion put to use
In my old griefs, and with my childhood's faith.
I love thee with a love I seemed to lose
With my lost saints, — I love thee with the breath,
Smiles, tears, of all my life! — and, if God choose,
I shall but love thee better after death.[1]

The libertine approach to love, however, is not confined to uncomprehending and immature spirits for whom first impulses serve as the solitary guide. Immorality can appear in solemn form and utter warning tones with the apparent authority of science and all the consideration of humanity. Thus the English philosopher and mathematician, Lord Bertrand Russell, whose services were ardently advocated for the American public schools, has urged premarital sex experience as a test of compatibility for possible husbands and wives. Judge Lindsey of the Denver court has similarly gone on record in favor of trial or "companionate" marriage; and undoubtedly there are thousands of couples living in this loose form of union, with at least a partial persuasion that it is the modern, progressive, "scientific" thing to do. Writing to Judge Lindsey about this matter, Lord Russell declared: "My own view is that the State and the law should take no notice of sexual relations apart from children, and that no marriage ceremony should be valid unless accompanied by a medical certificate of the woman's pregnancy."

Easy divorce and remarriage, under due process of law, have likewise been represented as a sociological development in line with the requirements of the twentieth century. The marriage bond being thus reduced to a mere contingent promise and possessing

---

[1] *Sonnets from the Portuguese.*

only the sanction of a reversible civic recognition, the matter of sexual attraction and relationships would seem to broaden out to such a degree that the assignment of any standards becomes impossible. As a matter of fact, the multiplication of divorce and remarriage in the United States has reached alarming proportions, and the situation becomes more tragic with the public character of many of the personalities who find themselves embroiled in marital mis-adventures.

Added to this is the current barrage of propaganda for birth control by means of contraceptives, likewise urged as a necessary sociological development. Thus the supreme sexual act assumes merely the same physiological character as that of the solitary act, and is justified as an act of love. According to a statement of the Federal Council of Churches of Christ, sexual relations in the married state "have their source in the thought and purpose of God, first for the creation of human life, but also as a manifestation of divine concern for the happiness of those who have so wholly merged their lives." This is indeed a beautiful and true statement; but as it goes on, it proceeds to state that these two purposes can be separated, without blame, by the human agents themselves, and the act may be employed for its love significance alone, while the couple frustrates its more fundamental purpose for the creation of life. If an appealing motive is all that is required to sanctify a violation of the primary functional purpose of the voluntary sexual act, it is difficult to see why the same argument might not be applied to demolish the entire moral code.

Professional propagandists, of course, lift the entire matter from any canons of moral criticism. Blithely passing over such considerations as self-discipline on the one hand and generosity on the other, they point the finger of scorn at the large family as an evidence of "baby-spawning," and to prove the point even marshal their evidence at times from families of idiots or from instances in which poverty and disease have taken their toll. As a result of this insidious development, the American family has steadily dwindled in size; and while, as a result of fewer mouths to feed, there is no doubt that many people have more money to spend on their own clothes, food, drink, motor cars, there is good reason to believe that much of the so-called "higher standard of living" is a cloak for selfishness of character and irresponsibility of outlook, which may well spell decadence of the race and eventual national ruin. In a word, the business of clean, ethical living is not simply a mechanical matter of "purity" as an isolated virtue, but embraces a wide range and combination of virtues, of mental attitudes and practised determinations.

III

The rule of right living, in the formation of a Christian personality, therefore, requires not only a common-sense approach based on the recognition of sexual realities but also self-control in accord with the moral law in all its phases. Vigilance and personal adjustment are required, not only to conquer temptations of erotic perversion, but also to meet social dilemmas of an apparently casual nature.

Mental balance, broad interests, and balanced activities are thus required, as I have mentioned elsewhere, to conquer the luxuriant jungle growth of what are sometimes called "bad thoughts," but which for the most part are merely promptings of the imagination stimulated by an organic condition of the body itself and which must be kept under proper control. The natural purpose of such promptings is to secure the great underlying result of the propagation of the human race, just as the promptings of the appetite for food and drink are intended by nature to urge the individual to sustain his health. None of these promptings is "bad" in this sense. They become bad or good according to the objects to which they are directed and the deliberated purpose which they serve.

Obviously, certain thoughts or types of affectionate regard which a man might entertain for his wife could not be justified, if for another man's wife. Thoughts which a person might have in legitimate attainment of knowledge regarding natural sexual processes could not be encouraged merely to stimulate or stupefy one's mind or body to a kind of sexual orgy. Erotic images which nature might allow to pass across the mind as a reminder of the impulses of the flesh can serve no useful or good purpose if allowed to enter the field of unlawful desire or to serve as a means of morose entertainment.

Some persons are violently afflicted with meteoric mental storms of this type. Particularly during the periods of adolescence and again on the threshold of what is called the "change of life" in the forties, highly colored dreams of a Mohammedan heaven flash across the struggling brains of most persons. When this condition is coupled with physical debility or nervous exhaustion, the most obvious remedy is rest and a good tonic. When it arises in connection with mental stagna tion or dullness of routine, the answer is great variety of activity, outdoor exercise, and possibly some creative reading or useful diversion. Idling around the house is fatal at all ages. If the difficulty arises from the reading of suggestive literature, the contemplation of immoral pictures, attendance at risque performances, exchange of off-color jokes, or from the cultivation of secret vices, then the only solution is a determined break with the source of morbidity.

Premarital relationships in courtship and extra-marital relationships in all circumstances require for their proper conduct a corresponding consciousness of ethical principle and personal responsibility, high standards of mutual regard, and the exercise of self-control. Many a man of fine character has been ruined by selfish women whose conception of love is intimate indulgence of the flesh; and many a splendid woman has been imposed upon and dragged down to unfortunate levels by the importunities of men who have demanded the sacrifice of virtue as a proof of devotion.

Particularly in American life, where almost unlimited freedom is granted in the mingling of men and women, the development of self-assurance must be placed on the firm basis of a knowledge of what is right and what is wrong, side by side with a realization of the inclinations of animal appetites. Youth must be trained in the civilized social courtesies and taught to understand that these are not merely the trappings of respectability but also safeguards against human frailty. A mature outlook is developed slowly, first by cordial hospitality in the home and a reasonable supervision over hours and types of friends cultivated outside the home. In the school, good manners in keeping with the formality of sex are to be encouraged. The purpose and value of proper dress are to be emphasized. The amenities of dancing, the niceties of etiquette, the cultivation of social restraint are all lessons which must be taught deliberately by wise parents and educators if youth is to arrive at maturity with a clean and steady outlook. Too many boys and girls are left to drift for themselves, torn between abstract moral teaching and the example of practical moral shambles until they give up the struggle in total disillusionment and confusion.

Just where and how to draw the line between rational prudence and severity in this educational process is not easy to say. Temperaments differ so widely and human reactions to guidance are so diverse that each case must be studied by itself. Some boys and girls are instinctively restrained, even shy, so that the problem, if any, consists in drawing them out into social cordiality and developing the arts of self-assurance and poise. Others are, from early childhood, inclined to be unstable and sexually precocious and require much more care and patience. The same is true of the adult, so that what may constitute a positive danger for one individual may be no more than a casual circumstance for another.

For all of us alike, however, there are certain common considerations. We cannot allow ourselves, for example, to associate on a basis of social intimacy with persons of loose morals, to frequent public centers of low standards, or to place ourselves in circumstances which clearly violate social conventions, without running serious risks of character. Irresponsible automobile courtships, philandering with married persons, keeping indiscriminate hours, drinking unwisely, are all symptoms of the moral maladjustment of which our age is guilty. As undue liberties increase, attitudes and habits are formed which destroy Christian personality; and no one can say that he or she is immune from the common danger.

One of the most insidious temptations a person may be called upon to face, in this respect, is that of rationalizing immoral conduct, so as to make it appear to his or her conscience as something entirely excusable or even holy. Impulses of the flesh are thus interpreted as the commands of Mother Nature, which must be obeyed without question. The fullness of physical union between lovers is justified as the irresistible manifestation of a union of souls, which harms no one and which God Himself must sanction. And so on. This form of argumentation, like all forms of self-deceit, requires the support of one lie after another, until the chain of rebellion enters every department of life. The unhappy mental warrior begins to doubt the sexual integrity of everyone and frequently withdraws faith in religion and even in God. If one will sin, and in the course of human experience all of us are subject to temptation, it is better to transgress with an honest consciousness of wrong and of guilt. With this attitude, the sinner is at least capable of contrition and retains his sense of principle. But there is small hope for the cowardly, evasive mentality that starts with the assumption that it can do no wrong and therefore that whatever is done is innocent and right.

In marriage and out, the same rules hold. Considerate restraint must always accompany true love. Generosity and self-control are watchwords with men and women who strive to deepen their capacity for friendship and affection. And we lay this down as a principle: that God will not sanction licentiousness or perversion, no matter how allegedly pure the motive of the guilty party may be.

I have emphasized the development of the *internal* personality. This is of the essence of right, happy, and successful living. It means dependability, constancy, and thoughtfulness in men, without any lack of virility and courage. It means fidelity, graciousness, and trust in women, without any diminution of charm and grace. But by the same token, every interior virtue, as well as every interior vice, leaves its stamp on the external person, sometimes intangibly but nevertheless really and certainly. And there is none that so readily shows itself as the mark of chastity or its opposite. It may appear in the cast of the eye, in the arrangement of dress, in posture, in a stray word – but the atmosphere or impression is there for instinct to detect. Wholesomeness of personality reveals itself at a glance, just as looseness of morals betrays its presence in persons, houses, and even neighborhoods on the very surface of things.

It is frequently said that there are far more grievous faults than those of frailty of the flesh. This is undoubtedly true. More than that, strong passion is often found in persons of intensely generous instincts, and, as sublimated into noble action, may well be one of the driving forces of creative expression in art, literature, social uplift, and of religious impulse itself. History is full of examples of persons, like St. Augustine, who have turned their energy from the pursuit of sensual gratification to that of the highest ideals in the service of mankind. It seems clear from the Gospels that Mary Magdalene, before her conversion to Christ, was a woman of the streets and possibly the selfsame who washed the Master's feet with her tears and anointed them with precious oil while the Scribes and Pharisees raised their eyebrows in amazement and disdain.

It is true also that in His compassion for sinners and in His expressions of divine mercy, Christ never discriminated against those who had the misfortune of sexual frailty, but pointed out that all alike, and both sexes equally, are subject to the same standards and the same consideration. One of the most beautiful incidents related in the Gospels is that of Christ's courage and courtesy toward the woman who was accused of adultery and about to be stoned. "He that is without sin among you, let him first cast a stone at her," He said to the crowd of her self-appointed executioners, and while He stooped to write in the sand some pertinent facts, they crept away in shame. Then turning toward the unhappy woman, He asked, "Hath no man condemned thee? Neither will I condemn thee. Go, and now sin no more."[2]

Nevertheless, lest we plead human frailty as a justification for looseness, Christ has been particularly severe in His laws governing marriage as well as particularly generous in His promises to the clean of heart: "Blessed are the clean of heart, for they shall see God."[3] Two of the ten commandments are given to an insistence upon the divine will: VI. Thou shalt not commit adultery; IX. Thou shalt not covet thy neighbor's wife. Never requiring that which is above human strength,

---

[2] John 8:7–11.
[3] Matt. 5:8.

the Lord replied to St. Paul's prayer, "My grace is sufficient for thee, for power is made perfect in infirmity."[4] And to all who retain faith in His special institutions of grace, there remain the sacraments of penance and of the Holy Eucharist, as sources of forgiveness, guidance, and strength. No Catholic who avails himself of these means can complain that the Christian law of clean living is incapable of fulfillment or impractical in view of human nature.

Solid Catholic culture has produced a pure people, a sturdy and happy people, confident in the acceptance and practice of Christian principles individually and socially. When these standards fail, civilization disintegrates, domestic and national disunion appear, and suspicion and brutality have their day. It must be admitted that present standards of sexual morality, as publicized in the press, on the screen and stage, and as revealed in competent social surveys, are perilously low. The individual who wishes to keep his balance and develop his life in conformity with the rich personality of Christ will have to make a heroic effort. But this much is certain: successful and happy living means high standards and *clean* living.

---

[4] 2 Cor. 12:9.

CHAPTER 6

PERSONAL DEVELOPMENT THROUGH OTHERS

"Bear ye one another's burdens, and so you shall fulfill the law of Christ" (Gal. 6:2).

I

BIOLOGISTS point out two fundamental instincts in all living creatures: self-preservation and the propagation of the species. To these we may add a third, particularly for mankind, namely, the tendency to associate with one's fellows. We are all interested in the world of things – in art, literature, science, and the beauties of nature. To a large extent we live our own individual lives and crave privacy. But there is nothing quite so interesting to us as human nature, and nothing that can take the place of friends. Persons who rise from the ranks to eminence largely through their own efforts and initiative are sometimes known as "self-made" men or women. But the truth is that we are all dependent upon and indebted to human society for nearly everything that we have and hold.

This fact is determined, in the first place, by physical and moral necessity. We are conceived and born without any wish on our part, and we are reared from helplessness by our parents. Then we become subject to the influences of association with sisters and brothers or neighborhood playmates. Still later, we are shaped by the social forces of schoolmates, friends, business associates, and general influences as revealed, for instance, in newspapers, books, motion pictures, and the radio.

Personality, as the composite of individual temperament, outlooks, and manners, is largely influenced by social environment. In part, its complexity is due to this. Its native strength and weakness are revealed through social dilemmas, so that we do not know ourselves completely until we have matched ourselves with others and faced the realities of social life. A sheltered existence does not necessarily indicate what kind of person I may be or how I may act in company; my conduct in society is no proof of how I may adapt myself in solitude. Many persons feel virtuous and strong only when alone, and they flee the tests of social life for this very reason. Others feel contented only in the company of others and are restless and distressed when left alone.

Sound personal development requires a careful balance of solitude and meditation with the careful selection of social companions and influences. Both are necessary. Incessant social activity results in superficiality and shallowness. One must take time out for reflection, silent study, and prayer, just as the body must rest and sleep if it is to carry out its normal functions. On the other hand, no one is sufficient unto himself. The advice and example, the sympathy and services of others, are necessary for us if we are to avoid an ingrown spirit of hypersensitivity, selfish conceit, and fear.

Nevertheless, we must not stop with a merely assimilative phase of development, like sponges soaking up water. Individual personality cannot be regarded as a constructive, mature power until it begins to exercise itself through activity upon others. And the complete, well-rounded Christian personality, as the active principle of a successful life, must be founded upon the life purpose of doing good and being of service to others. This is not to be confined to abstract conception but must be reduced to practical terms in actual life and within the range of one's power.

Expressed in terms of Christianity, this program means the daily habit and expression of charity as the great law of the New Testament. Such was the constant lesson taught by Christ, the grandest of all personalities. "Thou shalt love the Lord thy God," He said, "with thy whole heart, and with thy whole soul, and with thy whole mind. This is the greatest and the first commandment. And the second is like to this: Thou shalt love thy neighbor as thyself."[1] Asked, then, for a definition of neighbor, He told the story of the good Samaritan, who befriended the Jewish stranger, after the latter's own countrymen had passed him by, as he lay bruised by robbers.[2] St. John the Evangelist, who knew well the mind of the Master, could do no better in interpreting the spirit of Christ than to repeat, "My little children, love one another."[3]

II

Where shall we begin this development?

As a daily habit, ingrained in character, Christian kindness and helpfulness must begin by development

[1] Matt. 22:37–39.
[2] Luke 10:30 ff.
[3] 1 John, *passim.*

and expression in the home. It is unfortunately true that we are often at our best with strangers, but find it very difficult to get along with our own. One cannot be sure that he really knows a person until he lives under the same roof with him or her. For those whom we have never seen before and shall probably never see again, we reserve our choicest smiles, our most brilliant remarks, our finest manners, our best dishes. Perhaps, at the same time we have only cracked plates, sullen silence or a mean-spirited and taken-for-granted attitude toward those at home, blood of our blood, who have endured us through bright days and cloudy, and who will stand over our graves to shed their tears, if tears are to be shed. Certainly it would seem that – no matter how glowing an impression I may leave with passing acquaintances or what fame and fortune I may achieve abroad – if my influence in daily life with my familiars is repressive and ugly, then life itself has been a failure.

A number of obstacles stand in the way of a happy and fruitful personality, both within and outside the home. They all represent human limitations and to some extent are shared by all persons. But they are sufficiently tangible to be recognized in ourselves as well as in others. If we have the courage to admit and deplore their existence, we can proceed to study their deeper causes and strive to apply the remedies.

One of the first symptoms of difficulty is that of the grudging spirit, arising immediately from the notion that one is being imposed upon. Sometimes this is no more than a manifestation of sheer laziness. There are persons who hate to turn their hand for others simply because they do not care to put forth the effort. The only answer to this is the stimulation of one's energies and a training of the will. I have seen grown sons and daughters sit around while the mother prepared the meal, served it, and afterwards cleaned the dishes, without their even offering to raise a finger. Children may resent being asked to do the little chores about the house.

Instances of this kind simply confirm the responsibility of parents and superiors. Children who grow up without learning to work or to perform those tasks that are requisite to their state of life will inevitably blame the overindulgent mother or father. I have known of instances in which girls of very moderate circumstances have never learned to cook or to keep house, partly because of their own evasive laziness, but partly also because a mother's love (and sometimes a mother's wish to dominate everything) evaded or avoided the process of teaching them to do things for themselves.

More often, the grudging spirit is a manifestation of "ornery" selfishness. Children begin by shirking responsibility. They hate to be called away from play to go on errands that mean sacrificing pleasure. They frequently refuse to share their toys with others, no matter how wide an assortment they may have; and they suddenly acquire a passionate attachment for some long-forgotten or unnoticed item simply because someone else has taken a fancy to it. The same spirit is native to adults who carry on the traits of childhood.

Sometimes the difficulty can be traced to an inferiority complex. When children resent doing favors, they have an expression: "Who do you think I am?" We frequently fear that the fulfilling of requests may put us in a position of secondary importance. At home around the supper table, someone may ask us to get a glass of water, whereupon we snap back, "Get up yourself. You haven't rheumatism." The reaction, of course, is based upon our conception of personal values. If getting the water might convey the impression that service means inferiority, we are not going to serve. Thus it happens that life in many homes is a constant sparring for position, an unwillingness to volunteer assistance, much less to grant it when asked for, with all the attendant meanness, acts of retaliation, and boycott. Not much can be accomplished this way.

Similar to this, in going back to psychological origins, is what may be called the nagging or scolding spirit. This vice may represent nothing more than fatigue or a run-down physical condition. Blue Monday, with everyone out of sorts and shouting orders, as we have seen, is evidence of this condition. But in every case, particularly when the difficulty becomes a chronic bossing of others in a sharp, petulant voice, we can see every proof of the familiar inferiority complex trying to conceal itself by the simulation of power and dominance. The recollection of a nagging disposition is like that of a clock which has become deranged so that it strikes twelve on every hour or keeps on striking until it is turned off. The nagging habit, however, can manifest itself in far more subtle ways than simple shouting. It can assume the form of unauthorized eminent domain and proceed to direct the lives and shape the activities of others to such an extent that only positive rebellion will remedy the situation.

In the home, the spectacle of husbands dominating their wives, treating them as they would chattels or clients, in a firm but condescending spirit, or wives browbeating their husbands, is as old as history. In this connection, I always recall the story of the man who had meekly endured his wife's assumption of authority for many years. On one occasion, when she was entertaining guests, it occurred to her that they might like to see a valuable vase which she had purchased and placed at the head of the stairs. Suddenly turning to her husband in her customary rôle of top sergeant, she ordered him to bring the vase downstairs with all possible speed and caution. The man did as he was told; but in attempting to combine speed with caution, he tripped on the stairs when he had descended halfway and fell the rest of the distance. He might have broken several bones, but in his collapsed state he still nobly held the vase aloft.

The wife, disregarding his possible physical injuries, shouted, "John, did you break that vase?"

For the first time in his connubial career, the man asserted his self-respect, and rising with difficulty from the floor, answered, "No! But, by heaven, I will!" And he did, magnificently.

What unfortunately occurs between husbands and wives can also appear between parents and children. There are some parents who dread the day when their offspring may develop wills and ideas of their own; and they do everything possible to postpone or prevent it. Some fathers like to regard their sons as only boys incapable of mature judgment or independent action, no matter how old they may be, and their daughters as unsafe, if out of eyeshot. Mothers likewise are inclined to coddle their sons far beyond the limits of common sense, to block their marriages, and to make life as difficult as they can for the daughters-in-law who succeed in decoying the boys away from the safe moorings of the maternal fireside. Interesting also is the situation in which mothers become jealous of their daughters and do everything possible to retain the spotlight for themselves, even succumbing to mild hysteria when they fear that their dominance is being challenged.

On the other hand, it is not altogether unknown that children have taken matters in their hands and decided to manage their parents. During the period of rapid growth and new, exciting experience, there is an almost universal tendency on the part of flaming youth to become impatient with the more conservative judgment of parents and to regard them as quite unappreciative of new conditions that have developed in the world. When this attitude becomes ingrained and the youth finds himself or herself an important breadwinner in the family, trouble begins. Many a parent has learned to take abuse of the most humiliating sort from such children and lived in fear and trembling lest a word of reprimand or protest might bring the roof tumbling down upon the parental head.

Underlying a good deal of this monopolistic spirit is the assumption that others are more or less incapable of managing themselves properly without our guidance and intervention. There are some persons, familiarly known as "kibitzers," who are constantly passing judgment and giving advice in matters which are none of their concern. They sit in the second row around card tables and tell the players which cards to play or which cards should have been played. They take things out of others' hands and show them a better way of doing the task. They rearrange the furniture in others' homes, show them how to bring up their children, and give unsolicited advice on how to manage one's husband or wife. Mothers-in-law and maiden aunts have been traditionally imputed with these tendencies, but the truth is there is something of the meddler and the busybody in all of us.

This does not mean that we should assume an attitude of utter indifference to the problems of others, but it does mean that we can spare ourselves a great deal of unnecessary trouble and generally save the feelings of others by a certain reticence concerning their affairs. A great many things are wrong in the world. There is, no doubt, much waste, inefficiency, bungling, and stupidity around us. But that is no reason why we shall always feel called upon to intervene. If some invividuals, or families, or nations love to quarrel and to wipe one another off the face of the earth, or to lead lazy and backward existences, we may offer the example of peace and intelligent progress; but before entering the fray or imposing our way of life upon them, we might well ask ourselves to what extent we have a responsibility and to what degree our intervention will prove beneficial.

It frequently happens that persons who are most concerned with the affairs of others and are full of suggestions for the community portray an amazing spirit of unconcern in matters which pertain vitally to themselves. Or, lacking ambition for themselves, they are quick to detect false metal in the ambitions of others. Untidy homes and the habit of ridiculing new ideas of personal or domestic improvement as "ritzy" are familiar examples. Women who take special care of their appearance before marriage sometimes lapse into a lamentable lack of consideration for their husbands and thereafter disport themselves in loose wrappers and bedraggled hair about the home. Husbands can be guilty of the same carelessness, regarding the home as little better than a stable and unwilling to make any effort that will make themselves or their homes more intelligent and progressive. This condition reaches undescribable depths when aggravated by drunkenness.

Under these general circumstances, it is only natural that children should develop away from their parents and even come to despise them. When friendly suggestions for improvement or domestic cooperation are met by the rebuff, "If you don't think this place is good enough for you, you can always get out," the home has lost its real value. As a result, many young people hate to go home. The streets, strange companions, and disgust with life itself become their refuge.

If we examine these indications, as spread through society in general, we may sometimes discover the special devil to be the spirit of envy. An overreadiness to attribute unworthy motives to active and successful people, to indulge in petty criticisms of details in their dress or manner, and to glory in their failures or belittle their achievements – these are warnings to all of us who are sincerely striving to improve our personalities. When we find a kind of passive resistance to the enthusiasm of others, a sort of implied agreement to keep conversation at a minimum and all activities on a dead level in the home, it is time to ask ourselves why we have allowed ourselves to become mean spirited. And when we begin to regard our friends as rivals or to resent their good fortunes, we must lose no time in broadening our viewpoint, even taking heroic measures to share the good things of the world with others and to serve as an inspiration to high endeavor.

A similar vigilance must be maintained against persecution complexes, which can plague the mind even to the point of insanity. I once knew a man who had served as a doctor during the construction of the Panama Canal. Much of his work consisted in fighting the pestilential fevers that were spread among the workers by malarial mosquitoes. He finally became infected himself and was driven to permanent insanity by the disease. During his last days, he lived in the frightful hallucination that he was being constantly attacked by gigantic mosquitoes. Persecution complexes can become even worse hallucinations than this poor man's mosquitoes.

We have to forget a great many things in life. If I am going to resent and magnify every real and imaginary slight, I can make myself extremely unhappy and gradually cut myself off from every friend I have known. Some people go through life, not with a chip, but, one is tempted to say, with a lumber yard, on their shoulders, defying the world to knock it off and cherishing every counted chip that falls.

Indeed, there is much more energy wasted and more worries are generated through this form of dubious mental activity than we realize. I seldom ride the city buses or streetcars without hearing conversations whose theme is the unfair treatment or "dirty deals" received from the office manager, some crafty co-worker, or an untrue friend. In most cases, the villain is discovered in his underhanded crime and is completely vanquished in such expressions as "And then I told him (or her) in no uncertain terms—." It is strange how we unburden ourselves, quite unfairly, even about insignificant incidents involving our dearest friends, as though we have been badly treated.

In all this there is the enjoyment of a luxury known as self-pity. Children glory in it. Not rarely the child who has been punished for some misdemeanor will like to believe himself sorely abused and gets his revenge by imagining himself as dead and neatly set up in a casket while the heartbroken family cry their eyes out in remorse. Adults like to rehearse to their acquaintances how much they are misunderstood at home; and as senility creeps upon us, we begin to complain that an ungrateful world, particularly those who are giving the best years of their lives for us, are doing everything to neglect us and make our closing years difficult.

III

The principle of social charity is so beautiful and constructive that a mere diagnosis of these ailments and shortcomings in character is usually sufficient to suggest the cure. Too many of us are living in darkened rooms of the mind, when a simple lifting of the shades would show us all the glorious light of the sun and the beauty of God's creation. We come to tolerate, to understand, and to love people, not by waiting for them to serve us, much less by giving them an opportunity to display their defects, but by assuming the active rôle ourselves and giving others positive reasons for tolerating and loving us. Nothing wins friends so much as an unselfish concern on our part. Nothing makes us so worthy of friendship as developing ourselves, our resources, our personality by a program of friendliness and usefulness to others.

For the development of this program, certain fundamental realizations are necessary. The first is the conviction that the home and the family are the greatest and most abiding joy in life – that the home and all life stemming out from it can be made what we wish it to be, if we are willing to do our share in the cooperative enterprise. Nothing is too large and nothing is too small to contribute to this objective. Our respect for the rights of individuals and consideration for their opinions and sensitive points must be considered. A certain amount of privacy for each individual, and privacy for the home as such against intruders and interlopers, must be included in this. A spirit of companionship and solidarity, where confidences are respected – no hanging of "dirty linen," so to speak, in the front yard, for all the world to see – is very important. This means that the members of the family must learn to conduct a reasonable discussion and conversation with one another, never allowing that most un-Christian of all situations to arise, in which one member refuses to speak to another.

Important also is the observation of the amenities of gracious living, such as orderly eating. Children should be taught to eat properly and to remain at the table until dismissed. The idea that "anything goes," with food slapped on an untidy table, the members of the family arriving and leaving singly as they please, with no sound or activity except that of reaching for food and animal mastication, may work out for savages, but it is hardly an indication of the breeding we are striving for. Special occasions, such as anniversaries and birthdays, call for special observance, which unfortunately many of us, in the rush of business and immediate demands, frequently forget or forego. These matters are too precious to be dismissed lightly. The time to send roses is when others are alive to appreciate them.

One of the finest compliments I have ever heard paid to a man was that he actually *did* the kind things that the rest of us merely think of doing. Before one can reach this stage, however, one must actually *think* of such things. Some persons are naturally thoughtful. No occasion goes by without their doing "the right thing," some little word, or gift, or greeting. They have, as if by instinct, what Gelett Burgess once referred to as "the educated heart." But for most of us, the heart must be educated by a careful study of etiquette and a taking note of what really thoughtful people remember to do. Kind thoughtfulness really functions only when it has become an ingrained habit, and habits are acquired only through repeated deliberate acts.

If I am determined to do so, I can learn to smile, to cultivate a pleasant voice, and give a cheerful greeting, as my normal expression. No matter how belligerent my nature, I can with practice learn to speak kindly of others even behind their backs (one of the surest ways of making friends!) and to avoid bitter arguments and quarrels. I can even learn to defer my opinions to those of others. Through determination and reflection, I can develop a broad spirit and cheerful imagination, learning to make allowances for the shortcomings of others and to overlook their petty forms of bigotry and small inconsistencies.

More than that, I can learn to give an unqualified

praise, not always seeing the fly in the ointment, but concentrating on the positive goodness of man and of God's handiwork. One of the most touching illustrations of what can be accomplished in this manner came to my attention on the death of an old gentleman whom I had known for many years. He had been stricken with a heart ailment, and, confined to his room, was able to see the world only through the window. Every evening he watched the young people of the neighborhood coming back from work, and during the warm weather he used to answer their greetings. He became attached to one young man, in particular, who came in to pay him an occasional visit. It so happened that the boy was in constant difficulties, at home and at work. Of an unstable temperament and uncertain habits, he had been giving his parents extreme distress.

Nevertheless, the old man saw goodness in the lad and was grateful for the little sacrifices the boy made to come in to visit him. "I haven't long to live," he said one day, "but I want you to know how much I have appreciated your kindness and consideration to me. It has been truly an inspiration, which has brightened my last days and made my whole life more worth the living."

These words were spoken sincerely and with feeling. The boy recognized their truth. This was enough to make him respect himself and to change the whole course of his life into something principled and fine.

When I go back through my life, I find similar influences that have been an inspiration to whatever good there may be in me. Kind and encouraging words spoken to me as a boy, the friendly, serious consideration of persons who might have dismissed me as hardly meriting attention, little indications along the way that made me wish to make something great of my life, *obiter dicta* of praise overheard from others that stirred my ambition to be worthy of the comment and confidence – these things have played a part, in many ways more important than formal education, in giving me a vision of life and filled me with conceptions of public service that I regard as my greatest assets. It would, I am sure, be very interesting if I were to draw up a list of persons to whom I feel most deeply grateful for good influences on my character. Some of them might be surprised. Some have been strangers, others apparently casual acquaintances. Even abiding benefactors and friends may not realize how keenly we feel in their debt, or on what occasions the spark leaped from the torch.

This thought should be worth something to persons who feel that they are not being appreciated, as well as to those who think that nothing is worth the while unless it brings an immediate personal and tangible reward. The grandest characters I have known have done what they have done because they believed in the principle of service. Too many of us are ready to discourage sacrifice with the remark, "What are you doing that for? You will never be appreciated." For truly great souls, good deeds are a creative reflection of their very nature and personality. The element of thanks is entirely secondary.

As a matter of fact, much of the world's progress has been accomplished against bitter opposition. Many a benefactor of the human race has worked in obscurity. Many a monument extols the glory of one who was scorned by his own generation. Christ Himself is the supreme example of goodness crucified. The meanness of spirit and the cruelty of the faction that insisted upon His death were unable to touch the grandeur of His personality or to weaken the love of God, His Father, for whom He shaped His will. And the Cross has become the symbol of human redemption.

Every day brings its opportunities of self-development through the recognition of human values and the cultivation of those friendly little acts that make life happier for others. Some of the most gracious personalities I have ever met have been simple and retiring folk. The secret of their charm lay precisely in their desire to be helpful and gracious. Their poise and spontaneity arose from the fact that they were thinking of others, not of themselves.

In this respect, one finds a close kinship between the simple, openhearted people of the poor and men and women who have deservedly reached eminence. It is only in the middle ranks of those for whom a little knowledge is a dangerous thing, ambitious persons striving merely to improve their own material and social status, that one finds snobbishness. The birth of the Christ Child in a manger and the heavenly song of the angels to the shepherds on the hillside are tremendously significant.

Is it not true, also, that persons of eminence endear themselves to the rest of us, not exclusively by their great attainments, but rather by adapting themselves, when the occasion warrants it, to little situations? The king who lends his coat to the peasant, the president who writes a consoling note to the widow who has lost her son in the war, the general who remembers the names of his corporals, the great artist who is glad to sit down to a bad instrument and play for his friends – literature and history are full of these incidents, because they strike a chord of universal sympathy and understanding. From them we learn to extend ourselves, to offer our talents, whatever they may be, without endless coaxing, and to overlook no detail that may be useful in the act of courtesy. Thoughtful people do not have to be told what to do, for the simple reason that they are constantly seeking, on their own initiative, to learn.

This is not to become a "handshaker," a bore, or a nuisance. On the contrary, it is to reduce to practice the genuinely Christian aspirations of a fruitful and expanding personality. It is to begin at once the realization of the eternal happiness, which faith reveals as a passage from seeing darkly to beholding face to face the Divine Presence Itself. The words of St. Paul reveal the fullest possible conception of human personality and salvation: "Bear ye one another's burdens, and thus you shall fulfill the laws of Christ."

CHAPTER 7

SLAYING THE GREEN-EYED MONSTER

"Again I considered all the labors of men; and I remarked that their industries are exposed to the envy of their neighbor" (Eccles. 4:4).

I

SOME time ago, I was invited to attend a family party following the baptism of a newborn baby. The first child, a boy of four, was enjoying himself casually, until his grandmother began to call his attention to the fact that he would no longer be the center of affection, that henceforth he would have to share the center of the stage with his baby brother, that indeed he would now take a position of secondary importance, that mother and father and everyone would be more interested in the infant just baptized than in him. The unhappy thought, with this encouragement, began to reach the point of a realization in the mind of the youngster, and he showed in his whole expression that perhaps for the first time he was struggling with emotions born of envy and jealousy.

It is unfortunate that initiation into the problems of sharing with others so often takes this tantalizing form. Nevertheless, envy and jealousy, as offshoots of the instinct of self-preservation, fall to the lot of every individual. They must be analyzed and watched with constant vigilance if we are to achieve anything like poise of spirit and a happy adjustment with our fellow men. Let no one say that he is exempt from either. The form may be different and the manifestations subtle and curiously disguised, but the tendency is there all the same. Even animals feel these emotions. Dogs will fight among themselves for the affection of the master and even nip at a child whom they feel to be displacing them in the affection and attention of others.

Strictly speaking, envy and jealousy are very different in the objects toward which they are directed, if not necessarily in the motives which prompt them. "We are jealous," says George Crabbe in his delightful book of *Synonyms,* "of what is our own; we are envious of what is another's." Jealousy may be described as the personal reaction to any evidence that something which I prize is in danger of being taken from me, or as an aroused fear of and antagonism against the force that appears to have the desire to hurt me or deprive me of my possessions. Thus a man may be jealous of his honor, or excessively keen of guarding it, if he has reason to fear that someone may attack it. A woman is jealous of her husband if she fears that his affections are being estranged or are in danger of such by another. A lover is jealous of the sweetheart whom he wishes to win completely. A nation may be jealous of its territory, its wealth, or commerce – in other words, apprehensive lest these possessions be taken away by a hostile power. As a result, jealous persons build up protective walls around what they have, or submit their friends and possessions to various tests to assure themselves that they are still in command; or they develop forms of resistance or sensitivity that ring a loud bell of alarm, so to speak, on the approach of any threatening force. Apart from the connotation of excessive and unreasonable apprehension, it is evident that jealousy is good or bad, depending upon its object. With such connotation, however, jealousy means an agitated frame of mind flowing over into passion that can do much mischief.

In such a state of mind, every act, however innocent, is magnified into something sinister animated by sinister motives or symbolic of an evil trend, so that those we love most can become the source of constant suspicion. Thus the foxy Iago warned Othello, working him into a frenzy of jealousy toward his wife, Desdemona:

> O, beware, my lord of jealousy;
> It is the green-eyed monster which doth make
> The meat it feeds upon: that cuckold lives in bliss
> Who, certain of his fate, loves not his wronger;
> But, O, what damned minutes tells he o'er
> Who dotes, yet doubts, suspects, yet strongly loves![1]

Envy, on the other hand, is always bad, inasmuch as it looks to the injury of another, by wishing he were less fortunate in some possession and seeking means of depriving him of it. The envious man bites his nails, not because he is afraid of losing something that belongs to him, but because he sees someone else apparently better off than himself. A woman is envious of the superior beauty of her rival, not that she believes it possible for her to achieve an equal beauty, but that

---

[1] William Shakespeare, *Othello,* III, 3.

she wishes the other were reduced to her level. A student is envious of the success of one of his fellows, not that he himself hopes to attain higher marks, but would much prefer the other to fail. Envy equalizes by tearing down, or achieves predominance by reducing others to a level lower than our own. Envy does not always achieve its object, for it is primarily an attitude of mind; but it afflicts its possessor with a mental nausea that apparently can be cured only by the actual leveling off or shearing away of the real or imaginary advantages of others.

To some extent, envy is like covetousness, inasmuch as it may be followed by a desire for the goods or the honors of another. But its real meanness consists in this, that it resents the fact that others have these things. The envious man rejoices in the fall of heroes, the humiliation of the successful. His warped sense of justice is constantly asking, "Why should so-and-so have more than I have? Why should so-and-so be singled out for an honor that I do not possess?" In the words of Cassius to Brutus:

> Brutus and Caesar: What should be in that "Caesar"?
> Why should that name be sounded more than yours?
> Write them together, yours is as fair a name;
> Sound them, it doth become the mouth as well;
> Weigh them, it is as heavy; conjure with 'em,
> Brutus will start a spirit as soon as Caesar.
> Now, in the names of all the gods at once,
> Upon what meat doth this our Caesar feed,
> That he is grown so great?[2]

Or, in the more colloquial terms of Peter Finley Dunne's character who beheld his associate marching

---

[2] William Shakespeare, *Julius Caesar,* I, 2.

with great splendor in the St. Patrick's Day parade: "Here comes our hero. Give me a brick."

In common usage, however, the two expressions – envy and jealousy – are frequently used without distinction, very probably for the reason that both attitudes spring from the same thought, namely, that one is being deprived or is in danger of being deprived of something that strikes his pride. A lover is jealous of his sweetheart, not merely because he is afraid of losing her to someone else, but also because he resents the thought of being made a fool of by her running off with someone else. A clerk is envious of the advancement of a fellow worker to a better position, not merely because the other thereby gains what he himself does not receive, but also because this inequality reveals him in a less favorable light, both to himself and to others; and this disequilibrium hurts. Better that this undeserving fellow should be deprived of his gains, the envious man argues to himself, than that I should suffer the inner and outer humiliation of being passed by. The basis of envy, therefore, may well be a jealousy of one's own ego or sense of importance, which is shocked by the recognition of superiority in another.

II

With these conceptions of envy and jealousy, it is interesting to watch them in operation. Of course, it is much easier to watch them unfold in the reactions of others; but if one is honest and sufficiently reflective, he can detect the same "green-eyed monster" at work within himself.

One of the most familiar evidences of these vices is the tendency to engage in small criticism and in the inability to give an unqualified praise. In fact, the development of a critical ability may indicate a meanness of spirit as well as a keen perception. Thus we frequently hear such expressions as: "Yes, she has a splendid voice, but such an affected manner," or "He is a fine looking fellow, but, of course, very conceited," or "She dresses well, but did you notice she always wears the same things?" "Catty" remarks, as they are called, usually give evidence of an inner envy or jealousy. I once knew a gentleman who grew furiously sarcastic about the idea of carrying a walking stick. As it developed, he had a secret passion to carry one himself, but never had the courage to do so among his friends.

Another evidence is the practice of belittling the success or the importance of others, particularly of those whom we have known personally and in more humble circumstances. Was it not Christ who said, "A prophet is not without honor, save in his own country and in his own house"?[3] His wisdom and miracles made little headway among those who knew His local background, His family, and relations. "How came this man by His wisdom and miracles?" they remarked. "Is not this the carpenter's son? Is not His mother called Mary, and His brethren James and Joseph and Simon and Jude? And His sisters, are they not all with us? Whence, therefore, hath He all these things?"[4] And, as the Scripture states, they were scandalized in Him.

In the home, this type of envy has the effect of reducing family life to a dead level, where initiative, alertness, and the expression of personality are outlawed. New ideas, ambition for self-improvement, and success in personal endeavors, far from being encour-

---

[3] Matt. 13:57.
[4] Matt. 13:54–56.

aged and applauded, are often looked upon with resentment as though such activity and distinction were unfair to others and an affectation of superiority which honest, decent souls should not tolerate. "Who does she think she is?" exclaims the envious sister. "Since when has he become so important?" inquires the envious brother.

In public life, the neighborhood, the community, or the national group is frequently more inclined to accept the words of a stranger than it is of a local figure. The man who strives for pre-eminence in a given field may often find himself branded as an opportunist, a "publicity seeker," interested only in material gain, vastly overrated, an upstart, or a snob, by his familiars or his near-familiars who see no reason why one of their own should be outstanding, or be regarded as outstanding, or allowed to become outstanding.

History and experience are full of unfortunate examples of unheeded, belittled, and thwarted talent and leadership. Undoubtedly the reason for the failure of many good causes and of worthy institutions and movements is to be found in the small mentality and picayune attitudes of those within the group who will not allow the development of outstanding leadership but devote their energies to the task of belittling evidences of promise and superiority or in imputing base and dubious motives to those who attempt to lead the way to higher things. In such an atmosphere, none but the most courageous and persistent talent can survive. Mediocrity is glorified; and men of genuine ability and aspirations learn that caution, discretion, silence, and inactivity are the habits to be cultivated if one wishes peace.

Envy and jealousy of this type can reach a special

piquancy in professional circles; and let us pause to remark that women are unfairly accused of being more susceptible to these vices in this respect than men. Doctors, lawyers, artists, teachers, even religious within the sanctuary, are not immune. Oldsters who lack vision and largeness of view, men and women interested only or principally in their own advancement, security, reputation, or wealth, are often likely to view with alarm the appearance of fresh new talent and ambition and to use various forms of sabotage to belittle and block the progress of the younger generation. Various motives can be made to serve the purposes of envy and jealousy and to see dangerous rivalry in others who give promise of success or who have already achieved success in our own fields. This was the line of reasoning of Brutus as he meditated on Caesar's doom:

> And therefore think him as a serpent's egg
> Which hatch'd, would, as his kind, grow mischievous,
> And kill him in the shell.[5]

Such jealousy for one's own position or envy of the success of others need not always be obvious to the person possessing it. There is such a thing as unconscious as well as conscious "spite." These deeper, subconscious wellsprings of action are often the most dangerous and may be present in the most pious as well as in the most openly wicked. Many good people would be heartily ashamed of themselves if they could bring to the surface and analyze the motives that have caused them to work mischief on others. But, ranging all the way from the most secret wellsprings of action to the most candid, open expressions of malice, envy and jealousy will manifest themselves, from sulkiness

---

[5] *Op. cit.*, II, 1.

of manner, a scheming mentality, and malicious gossip to "poison pen" letters, calumny, defamation, and even murder. The harm that can come unless these tendencies are recognized and bridled is limitless. It was envy that crucified Christ.

One of the most familiar forms of jealousy, of course, is that which exists between lovers. Nearly every courtship passes through the jealous phase, in which each of the interested parties must know where the other is on all occasions, with whom the other has been and why, with a considerable amount of inner torment until all episodes have been explained to complete satisfaction. Some people never emerge from this condition, so that married life continues as a form of constant bondage, with protracted explanations and alibis for every move.

There are some wives, for example, who make a practice of pursuing their husbands, by sudden appearances and frequent telephone calls, even in the midst of business conferences, creating an atmosphere of exasperation and disgust. There are some men, on the other hand, who resent the idea of their wives' engaging in any form of social life outside the home and resent their wives' friends, particularly those of long standing before marriage, to such an extent, whether men or women, that continued relationships with them become decidedly embarrassing. These attitudes are sometimes brutally open and at other times are so subtle that it is difficult to localize them to a particular incident or to call them by their right name; but the results in unhappiness and frequent disruption of the home are tangible enough.

This form of jealousy can flourish also between

friends. When a person begins to monopolize the time of another, to cut in on his privacy, to assume that the other has no other friends or to endeavor to keep them outside the sacred circle, to appear on the doorstep whenever the other is leaving the house, to shoulder through any group and claim the other's exclusive attention, and in general to make it known or to give the impression that all others had better step aside, then the symptoms are well on the march; and it is but a question of time before the friendship will explode.

Conversely, two close friends, particularly those whose common interests or whose temperaments are not genuinely sympathetic, will find their attachment cooling if jealousy in the form of a rival ambition begins to develop. The condition for some friendships, it would appear, is that neither or none of the parties forge ahead or win any special mark of distinction. The cultivation of new friends, the development of new interests, or the smile of superior good fortune is more than some people can endure in their friends. The feeling of neglect and self-pity, and caustic remarks impugning the other's motives and integrity begin to shake the edifice of good understanding; and it is not long before lasting separation has been achieved.

III

How can the well-planned personality avoid those pitfalls? Pitfalls they are, both for personal happiness and peace of mind as well as for the welfare and advancement of society. Jealous and envious people live in a world of inner agony, of mental claustrophobia, of disordered and painful fantasy. And the harm they do, not only in the warping of their own lives and personalities but also in creating a warped atmosphere of intrigue, mistrust, and fear, is incalculable.

Both envy and jealousy, it may be repeated, are deformations of the instinct of self-preservation. By autosuggestion and the encouragement or example of others, an attitude of mind can be developed in which one is constantly on guard, constantly suspicious, always ready to plant hidden explosives and erect barriers of barbed wire, as though life were nothing more than a warfare of sinister elements for a survival of the fittest. To avoid the development of this unhappy outlook on life, it is obvious that the mind must be trained in the appreciation of certain constant values and by habit to face forward and upward, away from the incidentals of meanness and pettifogging that clutter so many lives.

This training must begin early in life. Parents and teachers should impress upon young minds the value of learning to share with others and the wrongness of begrudging others the good things of life or of desiring revenge for imaginary or even real hurts and slights. At the same time, there should be developed a capacity for admiration of greatness and goodness, not of the selfish or simpering hero-worshiping variety, but with a real sense of participation in these values and with an appreciation of the worth of supporting others in their forward movement.

There are various ways of encouraging and developing these attitudes. Children should be taught to share their playthings to a reasonable extent with their playmates. They should be discouraged from mean criticism of others, such as accusing others of being "teacher's pet," and, more important still, they should be spared the example of envious and back-biting talk by their elders within the family circle. There is no point in prodding children with invidious comparisons, by tantalizing them with the alleged superiority of others, as in the familiar "Why don't you be like so-and-so?" Rather, the course to take is the setting of certain standards to be aimed for, as such, and the encouragement of self-reliance and a rational self-confidence. Persons who are self-reliant and who keep their attention centered on certain standards and objectives, as worthy of pursuit, are not likely to fall into the vices of envy and jealousy. The latter are the sins of introverts, trying to compensate for their own sense of inadequacy and lack of forcefulness.

A wise program of reading in biography or works of an inspirational character of real merit is also of value, for adults as well as for children. The objective should be the development of a nobility of mind, a certain detachment from partisanship, the power to stand apart and above the scene, to allow for perspective in human affairs, and a spirit of tolerance and understanding in the emotional fluxes and the conflicting ambitions of others. Persons who are inclined to jump into every fray, to act as judge and executioner, cannot do better than to study the attitude of Christ with the woman taken in adultery. "He that is without sin among you," said He, "let him first cast a stone at her."[6]

In helping others to achieve self-reliance, one makes the same gain for himself. One of the most unfortunate spectacles in life is that of the parent who cannot tolerate the thought of his or her children's ever reaching a point of self-reliance and independence. Such people would rear their children as perpetual infants, hot-

[6] John 8:3–11.

house products unable to exist in an open and free atmosphere. Instead of being a judicious guide toward maturity, their protecting hands become so heavy as to crush to death. The child emerges into youth and the youth into manhood or womanhood carrying the chain of parental resentment, super-vigilance, suspicion, and repression. A barrage of questions surrounds every activity. Such parents, as we have already noted, recline into old age complaining of neglect and ingratitude by their children and still demanding more in the way of self-abnegation and service, no matter how much is done in their behalf – a proof that they themselves have never known the meaning of self-reliance.

An interesting fact about envy and jealousy is precisely that these vices are a manifestation of personal weakness and therefore crop out in a clinging attitude as well as in sabotage with respect to others. It is always a manifestation of weakness to build a wall around one's children or to pursue friends to a point where others are denied access to them or they are deprived of time or opportunity for access to others. He or she is a weak teacher who endeavors to hold students down from surpassing the master, as though such excellence were disloyalty. He is a poor organizer who suppresses all initiative, as though new ideas, new blood, new impetus could lead only to disruption and disaster.

So far as organizations are concerned, the personal element of interest and leadership is of the utmost importance, but where the personal element becomes so dominant that the organization is only an adjunct to it, the soundness and permanency of the unit are questionable. The founder of a movement or of an organization who is so jealous of his command that he is unwilling to delegate authority or to allow for the interchange of opinion and advice, ends by failing to develop a body capable of surviving him. One of the poorest compliments that can be paid a leader is to say that his organization cannot get along without him. Such organizations, by process of inbreeding and atrophy, grow old, wither up, and die. Younger men and women of zeal and fresh outlook are repelled by the atmosphere of caution and repression that breeds envy and jealousy, and they leave in disgust or lose interest in the cause. Meanwhile, the "old guard," so to speak, with overzealous attachment to their personal stake in the matter, refuse to budge or they hold on to power by stirring up dissension, again by the method of envy and jealousy, until the day of reckoning. Such has been the fate of far too many worthy enterprises.

Experience of this kind should lead one to a further conclusion, namely, a healthy distrust of one's motives as associated with dealing out justice to others or in justifying one's attitudes of dislike or distrust of others. Normally, we dislike those whom we have wronged or those whom we should like to do evil to. We can easily find all kinds of excellent reasons for justifying our remarks or actions which are of a nature that reflects unfavorably upon others or serves to limit their opportunities or to cast doubt upon their character or qualifications. It is remarkable how sympathy or the lack of sympathy can place totally different interpretations upon the same act. Honesty with self, plus a minimum of reflection, will convince us that our alleged lofty attitudes and our keen sense of analysis and justice are often no more than a cloak for contemptible envy and jealousy on our part.

Conversely, we have to be on our guard against oversensitiveness to the reactions of others or to the development of a persecution complex, which interprets our own failures invariably as the result of envy and jealousy on the part of others. Such rationalization makes it impossible for us to come to grips with reality. False pride thus pictures the world as in a conspiracy against us. We find ourselves surrounded by a pigmy society from which there is no escape except that of recrimination and self-pity. Oversensitive people, introverts, lock themselves up from family, friends, and community; or their constant weeping on the shoulders of others, if they are inclined to give expression to their grief, makes people flee from their sad stories of frustration.

Largeness of mind, generosity of purpose, readiness to serve in a public cause without private gain or glory, a spirit of forgiveness and oversight of petty wrongs, and constancy of endeavor in that which is right — these must all be part of a personality that would aspire to be truly Christian. In this picture there is no place for bitterness, no morose brooding over personal wrongs, no scheming for revenge, no intriguing to pluck the feathers from the wings of others who might soar higher than we.

In the words of Browning's *Rabbi Ben Ezra,*

Rejoice we are allied
To that which doth provide
And not partake, effect and not receive!
A spark disturbs our clod;
Nearer we hold of God
Who gives, than of His tribes that take, I must believe.

Or of his *Patriot,*

Thus I entered, and thus I go!
In triumphs, people have dropped down dead.
"Paid by the world, what dost thou owe
Me?" — God might question; now instead,
" 'Tis God shall repay: I am safer so."

This detachment of spirit, by which a man labors for an ideal, rather than for a material reward, is not easy to achieve. Nor is it always easy to pool one's resources with others toward a common end, sharing primarily in the satisfaction of a work well done rather than in the achievement of personal ambition or in the recognition that comes with personal victory. On the contrary, as life marches on, the repeated experience of double dealing in those we trusted, the disillusionment of selfish motives that suddenly rise to the surface, the hardness and cruelty of competition that will use any means to achieve its ends, may have the unfortunate effect of making us cynical of the legitimate aspirations of others, resentful of their successes, and sour in spirit against the natural joy of our fellow man even in his well earned triumphs.

To be a good loser is an evidence of great moral character. To be able to step aside for others to carry on the work when our own shoulders become weary may sometimes mean the difference between the success or the failure of a worthy cause to which we have pledged ourselves. To rejoice in the achievements of others is never to lessen our own personal stature, but is rather to add the best elements of our own forces to that which is good and great. If we cannot always have life or society on our own terms, we can recognize at least that we are in a stronger position of command by exercising our faculties of admiration, appreciation, and encouragement than by venting our spleen upon that which we may dislike or by allowing our anger and disappointment to dominate our activity.

"Nothing can work me damage," wrote St. Bernard, as quoted by Emerson in his memorable essay on *Compensation,* "except myself; the harm that I sustain I carry about with me, and never am a real sufferer but through my own fault." Jealousy and envy are a real form of suffering, a needless burden, a psychological baggage, which the Christian personality will learn to put aside and thus to walk with lighter, firmer, and more joyous tread.

CHAPTER 8

FAMILIAR OPPORTUNITIES

"Justice and Peace have kissed" (Ps. 84:11).

I

IN THE whole realm of human affairs there is not to be found a more beautiful or genuinely satisfying picture than that of a tranquil domestic circle. The story is classic of the Roman matron who during a discussion of gems and personal ornaments proudly exhibited her sons as the most beautiful jewels in her life. From time immemorial, the family has been the prop of the state and the most substantial boast of every self-respecting community. Like all delicately balanced ensembles, however, most families are put together, and held in a bond approximating harmony, with considerable difficulty.

The old family group photographs with the father and mother surrounded by their children, carefully graded according to size or sex, perfectly laced and groomed and polished, and each with a sanctimonious smile for the edification of future generations, have always seemed to leave great scope for the imagination. How many hours and tears were spent by the mother and elder daughters in arranging all those ringlets and tying those ribbons, and how much reluctant energy and paternal insistence were given to shining the multitude of shoes. Meanwhile the father stamped and fumed around the house, with exasperation at the delay. There were many last minute jabs of the mother's handkerchief moistened with the lips to purge away unsuspected or newly acquired dirt spots on the various younger members. Finally came the assembly in the studio and the awful silence of the moment when the bulb of the camera was released. Then pandemonium broke loose again. This description may be slightly exaggerated, but it recalls something of the refining process, commonly known as rubbing elbows, by which most of us come to the use of reason and discover that getting along with others under the same roof is one of the more difficult of the arts.

There are three questions which every girl in love puts to her lover on all possible occasions. She insists on knowing whether he loves her, whether he loves her a great deal, and whether it will be forever. Upon receiving a solemn assurance that such are the incontrovertible facts, she proceeds to guarantee her hold on him by demanding to know if he will ever forget what he has said. He replies that he never will. But life is full of queer jokes and strange developments. The effect of moonlight and the mysterious ardor of romance need a certain amount of calculating common sense for anything like permanence, and the unforseen reactions of most people to such prosaic things as time, hot spells, bad stomachs, perennial familiarity, and differences of political opinion, must be corrected by the studied virtues of patience, sympathy, and restful silence.

In print or picture, the upsetting of domestic peace can appear very amusing. To the parties concerned, however, the scene is anything but humorous. A few simple calculations will convince any thoughtful observer that for every marriage ending in the divorce court, there are scores of others existing in continual and tragic disunion of heart and spirit. The solution in most cases is simple. The source of difficulty may in reality be nothing more than a lack of reflective patience or of a grain of humor over trifles.

The husband comes home for dinner and discovers that it is not ready. His wife has been delayed at a bridge game. He insists that she had no business to be late. She must have realized how hard he has been working, how much worry he has had to endure over failing business, how voracious his appetite has become, all for the sake of her unappreciating self. When she realized what time it was, she should have upset the card table, and dashed madly home to succor her exhausted spouse.

Perhaps the conversation takes another turn. It is the husband who is late. The potatoes are cold. He doesn't like cold potatoes. Neither does his wife. He should have let all work drop on the hour and come home in time. He owed it, if not to himself, or to his wife, at least to the potatoes, to have been home to devour them when they were hot and hospitable.

Physicians tell us that a quiet, cheerful disposition is the best aid to digestion, but many of us select meal time as a favorite period to become upset temperamentally; and for many families, the dinner table is memorable principally as the scene of many battles. What should normally be an opportunity for relaxation and enjoyment, for the exchange of thoughts and experiences, becomes a period of intolerable tenseness and silence. As a result, many families never come to know and truly appreciate one another. The inner and positive development of individuals thus remains a secret process to those within the inner circle, and we come to know our own principally in terms of their faults and shortcomings. Nothing really good or outstanding is expected. Our attitudes become mean and warped, and we find ourselves degenerating into habits of complaint or resentment, which break out into speech.

Nothing makes life more miserable than the ready tendency to nag on the slightest provocation. Some mothers are continually complaining about the unruly conduct of their children. If the children were permitted to express their reactions, they would undoubtedly have many salutary lessons to teach their parents. Many indeed, do express their reactions, by developing trigger tempers, quarrelsome spirits, and a tendency to waste their lives in concentration on petty annoyances. Mothers who nag their children for every little trifle can expect a corresponding loss of respect. What is more, parents who curse and swear at their children can reasonably be prepared to receive the same compliments from their offspring. After all, most parents pose as models for their children.

A great deal of harm is done also by the constant threat of punishment from the father. "Just wait till your father comes home," is an expression that should be discontinued. Many a boy has grown up in mortal terror of his father, whom he has been taught to regard in terms of the official flogger, and has missed that companionship and confidence which he needed during the most critical period of his life.

Another form of parental shrewishness most absurd and distasteful to children is the selection of some living model whose exemplary conduct is recalled whenever a situation seems in need of improvement, with the remark, "Why can't you be like so-and-so?" Nothing, to repeat, could so arouse the passionate determination not to be like so-and-so.

The threat habit may be the product of a badly organized nervous system which requires a physician's care or it may be founded on the mental error of expecting and demanding more from people than they can reasonably give or even have within their power. Some parents require everything from their children, and think that because they have given the best years of their life to rear and educate them, that the children should obey their slightest and most irrational wish, all from the motive of love. There are children who are educated like slaves, with the intention that they shall return to the ancestral fireside and burn out their virginal lives in petty services to their progenitors. Some fathers who are death against smoking consider that all of love's labor has been lost, if their sons, who may have made the most of all their advantages, insist on having a pipe of tobacco.

One of the keenest joys of parents is to see the development and fruition in succeeding generations of the ambitions which cannot be fully realized in their own lives. The identity of the parent is extended into the activity of the sons and daughters and still farther into the grandchildren. Besides indicating a lack of vision and a downright selfishness, it may be a refined type of cruelty for parents to extend advantages to their children and then deny them the opportunity of pursuing the vistas that have been opened before them. Many a tragedy of broken lives may be read in the refusal of parents to move away from undesirable communities, when they could easily do so, withholding from their children the social contacts and cultural advantages to which they are entitled. Such selfishness sometimes takes the opposite course. Some children find themselves forced into careers and situations for which they have no desire or preparation, even perhaps to the threshold of a profession which it utterly hateful to them, only to discover at the last moment that they must exercise their own judgment against all odds.

It is probably in meddling with affairs about which we know little or in which we have no right that we render ourselves the greatest nuisance to mankind. There are people who may have been born with a constitutional disposition for "kibitzing," or they may have acquired an inrooted habit because no one has had the courage to point out to them the universal distaste for meddlers.

If the matter ended at the point where they could be politely dismissed with a kind but firm remark, no one would be any the worse off. Unfortunately there are often ties of relationship or yokes of obligation which render such simple formality out of the question, and then they proceed to enter into one's life and personal concerns like the camel entering the tent of the hospitable Arab.

There are few mothers who consider any girl good enough for their sons. The theory seems to be that once a boy, always a boy; and a boy always needs the mother's hand. There are mothers who resent particularly that any woman should alienate their sons' affections, so that the latter should seem to love their wives more than their mothers, or that the wife should so dominate in the home that the mother should be considered only a visitor. The slightest sign of disorder in the new domestic establishment, such as an accumulation of unwashed dishes on the kitchen sink or the presence of dust on the parlor table, is often enough to confirm the worst suspicions of such maternal mentors, and unless the young wife has the courage to draw the line in no uncertain terms, she may find herself rapidly sinking to the level of an undesirable boarder or inefficient apprentice in a secondary establishment of her husband's parent.

Sometimes the matter turns about, and mother and daughter band together in a protective association against the young man whom the daughter has been "duped" into marrying. They soon discover from what inferior stock he has sprung. The mother warns her daughter not to be a slave to her husband as she herself has been. As a result of the various implications of such advice, the husband may find himself reduced to a series of cold dinners or a self-help program on the days which his wife takes off. Perhaps he is faced with the program of a childless marriage, when he craves the joy at least of perpetuating the family name.

Sisters-in-law, brothers-in-law, and educated aunts are not seldom blessed with missionary vocations of the same general drift, and from dropping in on the newly wedded couple from time to time, they gradually take over the management of the house, the arrangement of the furniture, the formation of character in the children, and the running of the automobile, or they settle into the freer and easier existence of regular boarders. There is an old saying to the effect that when one marries, he espouses a good deal of the landscape. Many marriages that might have been ideally happy have been ruined because of earthquakes, chasms, and landslides caused by relatives in the foreground.

Our general tendency to lend a helping hand is frequently animated, more than we suspect, by selfish motives, and the solutions which we offer for the improvement of the world are often no more than an exercise of our critical faculties to call attention to the flaws of others and to magnify our own virtues. Of course, there is such a thing as justifiable and helpful criticism; and even small talk with a touch of scandal may unwittingly serve a good policing purpose. We are all afraid to have people talk about us unfavorably, and undoubtedly most of us are kept as good as we are and prevented from doing scandalous things by the fear of what people will say.

The danger of the critical faculty is that it can develop like a tobacco or alcoholic habit, or like a passion so keen that it requires constant gratification and in increasing measure, until casual facts do not satisfy it; then blemishes and scandals must be ferreted out and even created, if necessary. Some people live with either their ear to the ground or their eye at the keyhole, listening for the slightest rustle or looking for the smallest movement that might be interpreted luridly and delivered to a public of idle or prurient imaginations. The consciousness of innocence is not an entirely satisfying consolation if one is aware of a conspiracy against his reputation, for it is true that wherever mud is thrown, some will stay.

One of the underlying reasons for a small and critical spirit is the possession of what is commonly called an inferiority complex. A little self-examination reveals that the reason some people bother our nerves can be found in their ability to do things we should like to do or in their ownership of qualities or access to opportunities which have been denied to us. Those whose hidden desires for romance puts them on the defensive against women are eaten up with scorn for lady killers.

Among the easier and more effective ways of putting people in their place is that of damning with faint praise and of carefully inserting a fly in the ointment of our compliments. There are few of us who can give an unqualified compliment if we feel any rivalry or tinge of frustration with regard to the object of our admirations. Women whose attention is called to the superior charm of another are tempted to discover that she uses rouge injudiciously or perhaps that a wind-blown "bob" is unbecoming to one of her age. Those with the honeyed faculty of attracting a circle of men in any social gathering are suspected of shallowness and sundry indiscretions.

It may be a surprising fact, but it is frequently true that the things which annoy us most in other people are nothing more than a reflection of our own shortcomings. If I am disgusted with the egotism of another and his constant allusion to the first person in no unfavorable terms, it is probably because I have an overweening desire to hold the floor myself. My attention is called to the stinginess of others partly by the recollection of my own excessive frugality on several occasions. We are all quick to detect insincerity and to note the *faux pas* of others if they have committed the same sins or fallen into the same trap as ourselves. After all, this is quite natural. The yardstick which I apply to the measurement of others has been forged from my own limitations. One reason many families fail to get along in peace is that they do not recognize the hereditary possession of certain shortcomings in common, and consequently they are unprepared to understand the law of give and take.

The most unfortunate aspect of the personal element in criticism appears when someone has something of serious concern to cover up in himself or to excuse, by attributing the same defect to all mankind. Hypocrites and those whose lives are filled with insincerities of various colors feel no qualm in misinterpreting the most insignificant actions of others and in fabricating a story where facts are missing. The purpose of this procedure is to construct a series of fortifications behind which one can retreat whenever there is a danger of a personal attack, and thus allow the mud and missiles to fall on a third party. It is something like having a bunch of straw men on hand, who can be demolished indignantly whenever one's own integrity is threatened.

Persons who are habitually unclean in their lives or dishonest, and wish to appear as paragons of virtue, proceed to "get things on" others. They like to hear scandal, and they like to discuss it. Anything that could possibly be twisted or construed out of its normal bearing into a compromising situation like something in their own lives, they are eager to know and to spread with a mildly affected air of contempt or of virtuous martyrdom. No one is safe from such people. It is hardly too much to say that to the impure all things are impure and to the dishonest all people are dishonest. Such persons, not content to see their faults mirrored in others, wish to project their own images throughout the world like false beacons to put the impress of deformity on everything they illumine and to call attention away from the source. For such persons, we may cry, "Peace, peace, and there is no peace." There is a final point where even a sense of humor cannot sustain us.

I once picked up in an old shop in Rome a seventeenth-century painting which the dealer declared was a representation of the visit of the Blessed Virgin with her cousin Elizabeth. I took the picture home, and on further study discovered that the dealer was mistaken; the subject was not the Visitation but an allegory of that beautiful expression in the psalm, "Justice and Peace have kissed." The disturbance of family peace is always due to some injustice, real or imaginary, and some compromise is always necessary. Where the injustice is real and cannot be remedied, there is nothing for us to do but wait in prayerful patience until God's hand shall intervene. Thoughtful and sincere people, however, can usually arbitrate their differences. In the vast majority of cases it will be discovered that the difficulty is, not an injustice, but a difference of temperament, a simple misunderstanding of realities, and a tendency to self-pity, with the illusion of injustice.

Justice is something bigger than merely getting every thing and every consideration that is due to us on every occasion. The pendulum of life swings back and forth, now favoring one person and now another. We have to wait for our turn and put ourselves out to serve others and suffer them, against the time when they must serve and suffer us. Even our altruism has to be taken under advisement with others. The world has long suffered from altruists whose idea of improvement consists in reducing everything to their own levels. The maintenance of peace means the mutual giving up of certain rights and privileges, particularly that of talking out of turn; and peace grows most secure in the silence of practical meditation.

II

Among our recollections of the Victorian era is that of the venerable front parlor. It was usually kept hushed and shaded and locked. It contained the family albums, the conch shells, and the what-not stands covered with dusty bric-a-brac. It was the wonder of the domestic establishment; but it was not for the enjoyment of the family. It was reserved for the entertainment and amazement of guests.

The old Victorian parlor has pretty well disappeared; but the spirit of its tradition lingers. We are still inclined to reserve our best service for guests. Our ample tablecloths, our best teacups and glassware, and the plates shining with pride make their appearance when strangers arrive to taste our hospitality. Meanwhile, the family must be content with the daily round of the second-rate articles; the mended tablecloths and those whose history has to be concealed by various stretchings, turnings, and reversings; the chipped glasses, the venerable cups that have been divorced from their handles, and the plates that have experienced a decline or fall. If one of the family carelessly overturns a glass of water or drops a platter, the domestic tranquillity is definitely ruined. When a guest does the same, he is assured that everything is perfectly in order.

A good deal of the same holds true in our distinction between "home" manners and "party" manners. An introduction to a stranger calls forth our choicest qualities. Our personalities thrill with the charm of the moment, and our outstretched hands are limp with the elegance of pleasurable anticipations. For persons whom we have never seen before and perhaps shall never see again – mere passers-by in the procession of life – our best foot is forward. For our familiar friends, the tried and true, and for our families, who have suffered and endured us for many a year, almost anything will do.

Of course, it would be a shame never to rise to special occasions, or to have anything new or extra fine to offer the guests and outsiders who pause for a moment, as it were, at our threshold. But, it seems much more regrettable that we should be reserving our most brilliant and joyous moments for those who mean little to us, while we have only a dull and uninviting program to offer those who mean most to us – our familiars.

Familiarity is a charming thing; and, for those who would know life and drink deeply of human experience, it is an essential beginning. Familiarity needs the assistance of a certain formality or ceremonial, however, to draw out its powers of sympathy, of service, of inspiration, and of endurance. Unless it is supported by a more or less conscious program of study in the art of pleasing and interesting, it is bound to collapse into that corpselike condition, where everything is taken for granted and nothing is achieved except weariness and disgust for the commonplace. The stale conversation of the family dinner table, as an example, beginning with the supposition that none of the group has anything worth while to offer, ranges from the condition of the weather to the latest scandal, and then lapses into a deadly silence or breaks out into mutual vituperation — unless definite outside interests are cultivated and introduced for discussion as part of a preconceived program.

To build up this livelier contact, the cultivation of vital interests and of a wide-awake attitude toward life and literature is hardly enough. There must be, also, a tacit agreement between the members of the family to take each other seriously during these moments of truce and not to bring to ground, by a constant spirit of banter, every attempt to elevate the conversation. It is rather disheartening to have each earnest topic and impersonal revelation booed and ridiculed. There is no surer way of reducing everything to a dead level than by ridiculing the person who dares branch into a subject beyond the scope of local ailments and current styles.

This refusal of brothers and sisters to take each other seriously underlies the tragedy of unhappiness that mars many an otherwise ideal home. The older members of the family can never forget that they have seen the younger ones as babies; and the specter of that pitiful inferiority must haunt all their condescensions. The younger members, however, have a different conception of it. Life is just as real for them as it is for their elders, and just as full of problems. They are groping for expression and for sympathy. They do not care to be regarded all their lives as the babies of the family. A normal girl experiences a decidedly pleasurable thrill the first time she is addressed by a discriminating person as "Miss," and a boy feels the same thrill, the first time he discovers someone who is thoughtful enough to realize that he has graduated from the "Master" prefix to that of "Mister." If boys and girls cannot discuss their interests and problems at home, without being put off or laughed at, or being taken utterly for granted, it is only natural to suppose that they will go elsewhere for the companionship and direction that they need.

Underlying this situation there is, of course, a good deal of selfishness and unyielding pride. Family quarrels are frequently no more than a desire of all parties concerned to be victorious on all occasions. Many a nasty argument which has resulted in brothers' or sisters' absurdly refusing to speak to each other over a period of years, could have been avoided by the same delicate acknowledgment of error or defeat that we graciously tender to persons whom we scarcely know. It is impossible to be in the right all the time. Even if it were possible, what a magnificent gesture it would be to step aside, from time to time, and permit our adversaries to enjoy the sweet thrill of victory that has been ours so often, provided, of course, that no principles were involved and no harm could result.

A certain narrow and amateurish spirit also can be seen at the root of family impatience and misunderstanding. There is a technique in maintaining an unruffled front and a calm mastery amid difficult scenes and situations, a technique which is developed, not so much from sheer will power as from the ability to understand the human causes that direct the attitudes of others. The unfortunate gulf that often separates parents and children can be traced to a failure on the parents' side to recognize that their children are in a process of change and development, and on the children's side to realize that their parents' conservatism is the result of long experience. It is difficult to express the poignant sense of helplessness which fathers and mothers feel when they behold their children carried farther and farther away from them precisely by the social and educational advantages which they have toiled and sacrificed to give. But it is equally tragic for the children to feel that in this process of development they have been carried into worlds of thought and mental attitude which their parents fail to realize and appreciate. A genuine balance of sympathy and mutual understanding can never come from mere callousness. It can come only from a delicate reflection upon personal experience in an effort to learn the needs of others and a willingness to exchange the best we have for the best that others, whether they be young or old, have to offer us.

A small amount of self-examination will reveal that, as a rule, our impatience with others arises from the discovery that they are unconsciously mirroring our own shortcomings. If we could learn to apply to ourselves the measuring rods that we disgustedly use for others, we should be surprised to learn how frequently they coincide. Undoubtedly the common possession of family traits is a source of mutual annoyance at times to the members of the domestic circle; and a recognition of their common origin may help to bring about a more generous spirit of mutual forbearance.

It is too much to hope for perfect adjustment of familiar relations. Physiological causes, such as nervousness, faulty digestion, or more deep-seated organic disorders may be the causes of unruly dispositions. These call for a doctor, so far as the patient is concerned, and perhaps for a heroic spirit of sufferance on the part of others. Crudities of temper which have been indulged for a lifetime cannot be softened in some persons even with the most gentle and considerate treatment. There are certain individuals who refuse to respond to the most extreme courtesies. God alone can understand such people; and in Him we must confide our problems, with a prayer for that peace of mind and interior comfort which make life bearable and worth the living.

CHAPTER 9

RELIGION AND MENTAL HEALTH

"The fear of the Lord is the religiousness of knowledge. Religiousness shall keep and justify the heart: it shall give joy and gladness" (Ecclus. 1:17, 18).

I

IN EVERY age, thoughtful men have been able to point to signs of a growth of religious faith and sentiment in society. Within recent years, the fear of God has been recognized and even preached by statesmen as the only sure and civilized sanction for law. More than that, the issue of contemporary wars has been raised to the category of a religious crusade; and, while the totalitarian and "aggressor" nations have called upon God to witness the justice of their cause, the advocates of defense for political democracy, at least in America, have in large part aroused public opinion with the argument that the defeat of the democracies means a deathblow to religion, which free men must hold dear above all possessions.

Despite these generous sentiments, however, there is ample evidence that religion is under fire throughout the world as a hypocritical and venal conspiracy against the dignity and independence of man. The far-reaching character of the claims and moral obligations of religion is enough to stir the bitterest forms of antagonism among various classes of men, some positively advancing substitutes for what they seek to destroy, others content with registering a protest against what they conceive to be unjustified and gratuitous impositions of religious law and authority.

Thus, religion has been placed under severe disabilities in some instances as a matter of national policy. National socialism in Germany has attacked both Judaism and Christianity as foreign to German racial traditions; and even Lutheranism has been divided according as its adherents have been willing to accept State control or have stood out for independence of organization and thought. Fascism, in Italy, glorified devotion to the State without necessarily eradicating religious freedom, but its fundamental principles cannot be said to be in accordance with those of a Christian society. For that matter, the so-called Liberal state, particularly as it flourished in the nineteenth century, watering down religious belief and expression to a private opinion and striking out against organized religion, could little be regarded as in accord with Catholicism. Although Communist Russia has been unique for its positive program of godlessness, the irreligious governments of Mexico attempted similar objectives for a time under Marxist influences. Something of the same manifestation was present during the Spanish Civil War of 1936–39, although the irreligious fury of certain elements in the conflict were the result of social insanity and confusion as well as of Marxist infiltrations and Anarchist principles.

One of the most subtle factors in the deterioration

of religion in the United States has been an entirely secular policy of public education. Freedom of religion has been interpreted as a complete ignoring of the religious element in character training, and a number of leading educators have taken a definitely unfriendly attitude toward religion under any form involving the existence of a personal God. One such group has declared: "We regard the universe as self-existing and not created. We believe that man is a part of nature and that he has emerged as the result of a continuous process. We reject the traditional dualism of mind and body. We assert that modern science makes unacceptable any supernatural or cosmic guarantees of human values. We consider the complete realization of human personality to be the end of man's life."[1] One of the signers of this manifesto "calls upon men to give up the comforting thought of the fatherhood of God," and to accept the idea "that they are physically alone in a terrifying and uncaring universe, and that when our little span of life is done, we sink down into extinction, the blackness and darkness forever."[2]

This does not mean to say that the denial of God's existence necessarily leads men to throw all moral conceptions overboard. On the contrary, avowed atheists frequently establish the development of human personality as their highest goal, whether this takes the form of the individualist superman of Nietzche or of the benevolent humanitarian primarily interested in bettering the lot of the race. "Our goal," according to the *Humanist Manifesto,* "is a free and universal society

---

[1] Cf. Reiser, O. I., *Humanism and New World Ideals* (Yellow Springs, Ohio: The Antioch Press, 1933).

[2] Cf. Reese, C. W., *Humanism; Humanist Sermons* (Chicago: The Open Court Publishing Co., 1926, 1927).

in which people voluntarily and intelligently cooperate for a common good. Though we consider the religious forms and ideas of our fathers no longer adequate, the quest for the good life is still the central task of mankind."

Nevertheless, it is a fact that the flight from the good life often leads to an acceptance of the first principles of atheistic humanism. Just as the mother of Salome demanded the head of John the Baptist because he upbraided her for an incestuous marriage, people who have lapsed into immoral situations frequently reason themselves out of religion and attack it as the enemy of human happiness. Everyone strives for mental peace, but this is impossible for those who, as Christ says, try to serve two masters, God and Mammon. A choice must be made, and what so natural as that a man or woman whose life is unclean or dishonest should argue that God does not exist, that religion is a figment of the mind, and that religious persons are either deluded fanatics or hypocrites.

The most abject of all the enemies of religious practices, however, is sloth. Religious thought and prayer, it must be admitted, require the expenditure of energy. It is much easier to remain in bed on Sunday morning than it is to go to church. Catholics are sometimes accused of cowardice for wishing to clear their souls by confession; but confession itself requires special preparation, special effort, and sometimes considerably more courage than its critics possess. Catholic laws of abstinence on Fridays and special regulations of fasting from food mean unmistakable sacrifice. In addition, the support of religious enterprises requires the expenditure of money. It is not difficult, in view of these facts, to understand why many persons solve the problem by branding religious practice as fanatical and denounce the Church as a gigantic conspiracy against their comfort, their time, and their money.

II

There is ample evidence to show that these various attitudes have produced disastrous results for religion in the United States. According to figures gathered by the report of President Hoover's Research Committee on Social Trends, in 1926 only 59 per cent of the adults living in cities of 25,000 and over were church members, compared with 66 per cent in 1906. The committee comments, "In view of the rapid growth of cities, this loss of ground by the churches in the larger urban centers is of special interest." The same survey points out that the Bible receives less than half the attention it had twenty-five years ago.[3] The Roman Catholic Church remains the largest single denomination with a total membership officially given as over 20,000,000, of whom some 13,300,000 are persons of thirteen years of age and over. Some unofficial estimates place the total number at no less than 30,000,000. To most Protestants and nonbelievers, the fidelity of Catholics to the practice of their religion is a mystery approaching almost the miraculous; but keen observers cannot fail to realize that there is a large leakage in the Catholic Church also and a dilution of religious ardor among considerable numbers, even in the larger cities where Catholicism has presented a strong front.

It is true that church wealth as represented in church

---

[3] *Recent Social Trends in the United States* (New York: McGraw-Hill, 1933), v. II, p. 1022.

properties, such as educational institutions, monasteries, convents, hospitals, homes for the aged, orphanages, office buildings, and endowment funds, as well as churches, has notably increased, outstripping the growth of church membership up to the year 1926. On the other hand, in the following years from 1927 to 1936, while we increased our expenditures for armaments more than $50,000,000, contributions to the church decreased by $240,000,000.[4]

In answer to the frequent complaint that church members are "bled white" by the appeals of their organizations for financial assistance, it is interesting to note that in 1936 the American people contributed a total of $593,000,000 to churches and church benevolences, with an additional $557,000,000 to welfare and character building. At the same time, however, they were spending $2,350,000,000 on alcohol and narcotics, $1,250,000,000 on tobacco, $1,000,000,000 on movies with another billion on other amusements, $750,000,000 on pleasure travel, and many other billions on items of luxury. If the sum expended on religious projects is compared with that poured out on crime, a still more unfavorable ratio appears of one to fifteen![5]

What are the American people turning to in place of religion? It must be admitted that much which occupies their attention is hardly more than one or the other form of escape from personal reality and responsibility. Part of the answer can be found in the colossal expenditures which I have just outlined. Amusements, games, parties, the radio, liquor, fruitless reading, the Sunday papers . . . these are but a few of the distrac-

[4] *Ibid.*, v. I, p. 401.
[5] Quoted from bulletins issued by the National Committee for Religion and Welfare Recovery.

tions and toys that people have mistakenly come to identify with the blessings of "the American Way," but which in truth are only a substitute of the shadow for the substance of living. There is, of course, nothing new in this process of cluttering one's life with various kinds of mental confusion. The French philosopher Pascal described the entire process in his *Pensées* long ago.

Equally anti-intellectual and escapist is the development of superstition and pseudo science of a mystical sort. Hundreds of thousands of people who have had the advantages of education are turning to fortune tellers and astrology as the guides to action. Reliable investigators have indicated that as much as $125,000,000 is annually expended by the American public in its quest for occult information, ranging from gypsy seers to mystic magazines, psychic consulters, ouija boards, and even machines which are designed to tell the future by the insertion of a coin.

Others of greater intellectual integrity seek for moral guidance and personal development in ethical forums, cultural and political lectures, club work, and materialistic psychiatry. The expression of one's personality, the development of one's mind, and the ironing out of one's spiritual difficulties in terms of experience and what are loosely called "human values" thus become translated into salvation. Thus, wrote Oscar Wilde, whose own life was an example of pathetic failure, "when we reach the true culture that is our aim, we attain to that perfection of which the saints have dreamed, the perfection of those to whom sin is impossible, not because they make the renunciations of the ascetic, but because they can do everything they wish without hurt to the soul, and can wish for nothing that can do the soul harm, the soul being an entity so divine that it is able to transform into elements of a richer experience, or a finer susceptibility, or a newer mode of thought, acts, or passions that with the common would be commonplace, or with the uneducated, ignoble, or with the shameful, vile."[6]

In somewhat the same vein, although possibly on a more intellectual and less instinctive level than Wilde, Walter Lippmann declared in his *Preface to Morals,* "Since there is no principle under modern conditions which authorizes the re-establishment of a moral code, the moralist, unless he revises his premises, becomes entirely ineffectual. To revise his premises can, under the circumstances, mean only one thing: that he occupies himself with the problem of how to encourage that growth into maturity, that outgrowing of naïve desire, that cultivation of disinterestedness, which render passion innocent and an authoritative morality unnecessary."[7]

Lippmann, however, has subsequently realized that this cultural or humanitarian naturalism is not enough to provide us with an understanding of our personalities or with an adequate norm of human conduct. At their best, all these approaches are but fragmentary. Some of them positively divert the mind from a solution of life's problems. Others fail to find the purpose and aim of human existence. Still others serve as a camouflage for sin and sloth. And all, taken together, are unable to come to grips with the challenge of war,

---

[6] Oscar Wilde, *Intentions* (*The Critic as Artist*), (New York: Doubleday, Page and Co., 1923), p. 235.

[7] Walter Lippmann. *Preface to Morals* (New York: The Macmillan Co., 1929), p. 209.

crime, social insanity, and economic turmoil. No wonder that Lippmann in a syndicated article, "Reconstruction of a Democratic Philosophy," has been obliged by straight and persistent thinking to come back, like many another, to the ancient conclusion that "there is in each man a final essence, that is to say an immortal soul which only God can judge."

III

Constructive personal development and mental health require a sound and courageous acceptance of sound principles. The first principle of sane living is that man is a union of material body and spiritual soul. The second is that man has a relationship and responsibility, not only to himself and to society, but also and primarily to his Creator, God. These two fundamentals and their implications are what we call religion. Religion is the foundation of personal and social sanity, because it gives the only true understanding of human nature and provides the only true answer to the meaning of life. In the words of the first message of President Roosevelt to Congress in 1939, "Religion, by teaching man his relationship to God, gives the individual a sense of his own dignity and teaches him to respect himself by respecting his neighbor." In other words, order requires some sense of finality. If the idea of God is abolished, it is impossible to place the pattern of life and thought on anything but a confused tissue of compromises and lawless impulses.

This is true in public as well as in private spheres. Fundamentally, our social problems are moral and spiritual rather than economic or political. External laws are of small consequence unless founded upon justice and accepted as such by human intelligence. Moreover, whether in war or in peace, it will be found that the principal assets of a nation are not its material wealth and resources but the moral character of its citizens. History has demonstrated this truth over and over again. By the same tokens, there can be no doubt that the Church and related institutions, functioning in their proper capacities, are pre-eminently bulwarks in safeguarding and developing the moral fiber and spiritual power of the nation. All this was admirably summed up by Christ when He declared: "Seek ye therefore first the kingdom of God and his justice: and all these things shall be added unto you."[8]

The application of these principles and the test of their value must begin with the individual. It is absurd to speak of the benefits of religion, if religion is merely a sort of impersonal and mass fervor. Not much is solved, for example, by lip service to the great value of religious freedom or by the group singing of *God Bless America*. Religion becomes a personal and constructive force only when it is an integral factor in character formation and in the development of attitudes on life.

For this reason, the only logical and complete conception of education is that which is exemplified in the Catholic school. The religious basis of this system provides the individual with a realization of his own inherent spiritual dignity and, as a result, develops a genuinely reverential outlook on life. One of the greatest difficulties experienced in the public schools, recognized by capable educators everywhere, has been that of developing courtesy and respect toward authority and

---

[8] Matt. 6:33.

one's fellow man; and the reason for this is precisely that a godless or neutral education lacks a sound basis on which to fasten and build a secure scale of values. The inculcation of democracy by itself can succeed only in producing a haughty sense of personal freedom and of mass action. Without the corresponding realization of rights and duties springing from the nature of the soul, it is practically impossible to avoid the cynical and braggadocio spirit that spoils so much of American youth.

As the editor of *Fortune Magazine* has put the matter: "Democracy is a spirit, not a form of government. . . . The basic teachings of Christianity are in its [American democracy's] bloodstream. The central doctrine of its political system — *the inviolability of the individual* — is a doctrine inherited from nineteen hundred years of Christian *insistence upon the immortality of the soul* . . . the American owes all this to the Church. He owes it to the fight that the Church put up during long centuries in Europe. . . ." A conscious realization of these truths and facts is the only thing that can keep a nation together in civilized restraint and in common consideration for the amenities of cultured living.[9]

Again religion shows its value in the development of personality by providing a rational and absolute basis of moral principle and moral balance in the relationship between the individual and God. The sense of moral guilt, recognized by religion, far from being an unfortunate survival of savagery and fanaticism, is actually to the soul what the nervous system is to the body. It indicates a spiritual injury and clearly proves that

---

[9] *Fortune Magazine,* January, 1940. Editorial on War and Peace.

mental peace can be purchased only by the moral peace of reconciliation with God. Psychiatric treatment which ignores the moral element in human problems can frequently do more harm than good. A troubled conscience may well be a healthy warning which should not be disregarded. For this reason, the Confessional serves a profoundly constructive purpose in restoring intellectual balance and mental health for the very reason that it touches the most vital of all disorders, namely, estrangement of the soul from the law of the Creator.

Moreover, religion provides the key to mental repose and consolation in its reconciliation of the human mind with Divine Providence as the ruling plan of the universe. Religion enables man to look behind suffering and death and learn submission to the greater wisdom of God, with a vision of perfect justice in eternity. In the great crises of life, the person of religious faith remains calm because he realizes that God is aware of what is happening, that He has an ample reason for permitting moral evil as well as physical distress, and that, as Infinite Goodness, with His program drawn across the centuries and on into everlasting life, He will see to it that what is right will triumph, what is meritorious will be rewarded, and what is wrong and shameful will be punished. With filial love and confidence the Christian prays: "Thy Kingdom come, Thy will be done on earth as it is in heaven."

With this comprehension, St. Paul declared: "Be nothing solicitous: but in everything, by prayer and supplication, with thanksgiving, let your petitions be made known to God. And the peace of God, which surpasseth all understanding, keep your hearts and minds in Christ Jesus. For the rest, brethren, whatsoever things are true, whatsoever modest, whatsoever just, whatsoever holy, whatsoever lovely, whatsoever of good fame, if there be any virtue, if any praise of discipline: think on these things . . . and the God of peace shall be with you."[10]

To some extent, these values are found in all religion worthy of the name. Therefore, the rule must be kindness and humane tolerance toward all. In a world defense of religion, we must unite on fundamentals with Jew, Protestant, and all of good will. But in their fullness and perfection, these values are to be found only in the complete revelation of Christ, namely in the Catholic faith and in its one hundred per cent exercise, practised openly and courageously. For this, no sacrifice is too great, if the mind is to bear its full fruit and attain its full stature.

IV

In line with these considerations, the art of successful living and the development of Christian personality call for the cultivation of certain habits. The first is that of daily prayer. Only in this way can the human mind be kept attuned to the mind of God. No time is better spent than the few minutes upon rising and again before retiring at night in formal prayer, commending one's soul to God, purifying one's motives, examining one's conscience, making an act of contrition, and begging divine assistance in living aright. Parents should teach this life lesson to their children as soon as the little ones are able to understand, and the habit should be carried through life as a matter of rigorous obligation.

[10] Philip. 4:6–9.

To deepen one's spiritual perceptions, the practice of daily spiritual reading is also most helpful. The thoughtful person will set aside at least fifteen minutes a day for this purpose. Every Christian should read the New Testament over and over again, not hastily, but slowly assimilating its word and spirit. Thomas à Kempis' *Following of Christ* is another "must." The *Confessions* of St. Augustine is also on the list of truly great books. An enumeration of worth-while spiritual books might be extended indefinitely, with this caution, that much spiritual writing is highly personal, so that what may be helpful and inspiring to one person may appear insipid and affected or may even be disturbing to another. It must be admitted also that a great deal of what passes for spiritual writing is hardly more than a poorly digested re-presentation of ancient matter which has been much better and more honestly conceived by the great masters. Spiritual reading, like any other kind of reading, should be carefully selected.

Religious development, like any other growth, must be subject to competent guidance and control; and spiritual reading and exercises, like any strong tonic, must be indulged with the same rules of common sense as are required in administering tonic for the body. The soul is quite as sensitive to spiritual stimulus as the body is to material stimulus. It can also be wounded and warped or diseased. It is quite false, however, to lay mental disorders at the doorstep of religion, as though religious interest and fervor were the cause of fanaticism or insanity. A mistake frequently made is that of confusing emotional manifestations with authentic religion, whereas true religion, although capable of arousing great emotions such as love, is fundamentally and essentially, on the part of the individual, a rational acknowledgment of his responsibilities to God. The fact that certain emotionally unbalanced persons are "queer" or "go off" on the subject of religion is no indictment of religion as such, nor should this be a deterrent to rational individuals from wishing to perfect themselves spiritually.

Very often the criticism brought against religious interest and intensity is itself based upon misconceptions or is in itself a sign of spiritual shallowness. The difficulty with most people is not that they are too religious but that they are not sufficiently logical and persistent in their pursuit of religion. For too many people, religion is only an external lip service and religious services merely the discharge of a kind of group obligation. In general, Catholics are far more faithful in receiving the sacraments and attending Sunday Mass than non-Catholics are in attending the services which are distinctive of their various sects. But Catholics, by and large, may still ask themselves whether, for example, they are hearing Sunday Mass as intelligently as they might, following the Holy Sacrifice word for word and act for act as it is said and offered by the priest; or whether, in going to confession, their examination of conscience is as thoroughly honest and their good resolutions are as basic as their desire is to keep their finances in a healthy condition and their personal appearance attractive. The benefits of religion are usually in direct proportion to personal effort.

What is true of the individual in the care of his own soul is equally true of the individual in relation to the needs of contemporary society. As President Roosevelt has said in his Brotherhood Day Address,

February 21, 1936, "The chief religious issue is not between our various beliefs. It is between belief and unbelief. . . . No greater thing could come to our land today than a revival of the spirit of religion – a revival that would sweep through the homes of the nation and stir the hearts of men and women of all faiths to a reassertion of their belief in God and their dedication to His will for themselves and for their world. I doubt if there is any problem – social, political, or economic – that would not melt away before the fire of such a spiritual awakening." And Pope Pius XI, who so vigorously preached social justice on the basis of man's spiritual nature, declared: "Social reconstruction, so much desired, must be preceded by a profound renewal of the Christian spirit."[11] In a word, social sanity depends upon the mental health of the individuals comprising society; and this can be assured only if the minds of men are turned toward the mind of God.

Whatever we can do by way of good example, in observing the laws of our Church, courageously acknowledging our faith, assisting those who have fallen away or are floundering in doubt, crushing antireligious slander and calumny, living life in accordance with the laws of God, is the best contribution that we can make to the world in which we live. The words of Christ to Peter are a most precious injunction to everyone who would keep his own balance and assist his fellow man in the same endeavor: "But I have prayed for thee, that thy faith fail not; and thou, being once converted, confirm thy brethren."[12]

---

[11] Pope Pius XI, Encyclical *Quadragesimo Anno,* "On the Reconstruction of the Social Order," cf. *The Catholic Mind* (New York: The America Press), Vol. XXIX, No. 11, p. 297.

[12] Luke 22:32.

CHAPTER 10

RELIGION IN ACTION

"He that doth the will of my father who is in heaven, he shall enter into the kingdom of heaven" (Matt. 7:21).

I

AGAINST a long tradition, the United States was drawn into World War I, pledging its last resources and offering the blood of its youthful manhood upon the battlefields of Europe, "to make the world safe for democracy." It was a high ideal. There was something of a missionary spirit in the lighthearted troops that went across the sea. It was like saving the soul of the world.

Today, after a sadly disillusioning and insecure peace, that dream of democracy reasserts itself with the consciousness of a crusading mission. But it is reared upon the debris of an unsound prosperity. Instead of the promised brotherhood, there grew up a universal suspicion. Experiments in constitutional government were brutally abandoned in many sectors for dictatorships. Proletarian movements have developed into military tyrannies. The device of direct action and of the bloody purge has supplanted that of majority rule with fairness to minorities. Democracy itself has come to assume various and confused meanings. So far as the principle of equal rights for men is concerned, we are still in the midst of a world struggle, "testing," in the words of Lincoln, "whether that nation, or any nation, so conceived and so dedicated can long endure."

What is at the bottom of this struggle? Is the ideal too high or impractical in the present stage of the world's development? Or is there a body of international influences that has selfishly set itself against the principles of individual and collective freedom which we believe are at the basis of personal and national salvation?

The answer to these questions is not a simple one. Every nation has its own peculiar historical evolution that bears profoundly upon its present problems. The social fabric of various regions, rooted in racial and economic factors, creates different types of national souls, so to speak, and calls for different forms of self-discipline. Mutual relations of the various countries, be they sympathetic or hostile, have resulted in the creation of various kinds and qualities of national or regional ideals. What might mean the salvation of one could end in the destruction of another.

Without these qualifications, the mere preaching of democracy is "sounding brass and tinkling cymbal." The theory of equal rights, without due regard for the inborn inequalities of men and nations, can serve as a pharisaical front for the worst kind of exploitation and oppression. The worst abuses of Liberalism have sprung from a distortion of the principle of freedom. Under the guise of equality of opportunity, there has been developed a kind of social Darwinism, with ruthless competition, enormous monopolies, and social enslavement of those whose "equal rights" were not sufficient to make up for their personal disabilities in the struggle for existence.

Mass movements, employing the same principles, can become equally inconsiderate. There is no body so intolerant as that which is bent on freeing the world in spite of itself and convinced that it can secure justice for itself only by force. Our own democracy has not been exempt from these confusions and struggles. Our march across the continent was effected in part by a questionable conquest under the banner of democracy. And our colonial rule, flaunting the mission of democracy, has not always made those human readjustments that are necessary if justice is to be done.

National salvation, therefore, and the functioning of democracy as a means to this end clearly call for two lines of discipline. One exists in the order of citizens to the state; the other means the control of relations between men and men. In both instances, liberty, as the Apostle to the Gentiles repeatedly declared, must be built on law.

Nations have their responsibilities as nations, and Divine Providence, acting in harmony with the natural law, rewards or punishes groups of men as well as single persons. In this collective sense, the state may be said to have a soul, and indeed a soul that must render an account here below. But all social considerations must verge toward the salvation of the individual. It is the business of the civic order to organize society in the order of temporal prosperity and provide a material environment in which the finest cultural values may be developed and safeguarded. But unless the spiritual character of human personality is to be denied, it is only in the individual that the soul exists as an accountable unit in the order of eternal salvation.

The exaltation of the State at the cost of personal moral liberty and individual spiritual responsibility is indeed one of the most serious threats to human democracy today. Referring to the term "immortality," Pope Pius XI addressed these pertinent words to the German people: "Whoever only means by the term the collective survival here on earth of his people for an indefinite length of time, distorts one of the fundamental notions of the Christian Faith and tampers with the very foundation of the religious concept of the universe, which requires a moral order."[1] Then addressing himself to the German youth in a matter of practical conclusion, he added: "No one would think of preventing young Germans from establishing a true ethnical community in a noble love of freedom and loyalty to their country. What we object to is the voluntary and systematic antagonism raised between national education and religious duty."[2]

The pointedness of these principles is evident in contrast with a statement of the Reich Church Minister: "National Socialism consists of doing the will of God. The will of God is revealed in German blood. This will of God is the Nation."

A great deal of fear has been expressed lest the forces of either Fascism or Communism undermine the liberal democracy and the cultural and religious freedom of America. There may be reasons for these fears. A more potent source of danger, however, seems to be

---

[1] Pope Pius XI, Encyclical, *Mit brennender Sorge, The Present Position of the Catholic Church in the German Empire,* cf. *The Catholic Mind* (New York: The America Press), Vol. XXXV, No. 9, p. 195.

[2] *Ibid.,* p. 200.

the development of an educated body of thought which regards men merely as units of a sociological body, with no further destiny than that of a comfortable earthly existence and no other salvation than that of freedom from exploitation and superstition.

The scientific approach to human problems must commend itself to rational men; but this humanitarian outlook, masking itself behind the title of democracy, when coupled with a mild contempt for religious principles or for morality grounded on considerations of a hereafter, presents one of the most dangerous half-truths that America has to face today. For one thing, it means the creation of a completely secularized state, in which even the motto "In God we trust" would be regarded as a quaint but groundless sentiment. Morality based on any other considerations than those of convenience or therapeutic possibilities would be considered to stand in the way of human happiness and social progress. Public worship would be viewed as a wasteful, if innocent, form of consolation. Religious education would be attacked as essentially biased and unprogressive.

The salvation of America, from a technical standpoint, must consist in improving industrial relations, removing the causes of disease by improved hygienic methods, establishing more cultural centers with greater leisure, providing better means of communication, and working toward international peace. But in this work of material development and human improvement, religion, as church leaders have repeatedly declared, must lend itself as a basic factor if success is to be attained. In his Apostolic Letter of March 28, 1937, to the Mexican people, Pope Pius XI made a pointed statement to this effect: "Facing the frequent accusations made against the Church that it is indifferent to social problems, or incapable of solving them, do not desist from proclaiming that only the teaching and the work of the Church, assisted as it is by its Divine Founder, can furnish a remedy for the very grave ills which burden humanity. It is for you then (as you have already shown your wish to do) to draw from these fruitful principles the certain norms to solve the grave social questions with which your country is struggling today, which are, for example, the agrarian problem, the reduction of the large landed estates, the improvement of the living conditions of the working men and their families."

In this work, religion must not allow itself to be brushed aside by a philosophy that knows no finality beyond that of comfortable living and the grave. Man works out his salvation in society and in the state. But society is not his own soul, nor is the state God. What alone can be termed immortal in America is the number of the individual immortal souls of its citizens. Peace and progress and prosperity may be indications of national salvation, but they are purchased at the cost of individual effort and goodness. The salvation of the individual immortal soul is measured not by the degrees in which it has tasted the benefits of society or extolled the glories of democracy in which the individual has been privileged to live, but by the answer man himself can give to Almighty God.

II

Do business and religion mix? Can the businessman afford to let religious considerations enter his ledgers and affect his profits? Is religion within its rightful field when it steps into the realm of social justice as though it were its own?

These questions have commanded a great deal of thought within recent years. Discussion does not yet seem to have brought about a total agreement of opinion. When the clergy stand in their pulpits and speak, for example, of the obligations between employers and employees or come out for a more just distribution of the fruits of labor, they are frequently reminded by members of their flock that the church is the place for religion, not politics. Practical businessmen, on the other hand, are often inclined to feel that the preaching of moral principles and idealism in industry and commerce has been overdone. Theory, they say, is one thing; dollars and cents, another; and the only thing that finally counts is what works.

Now, I think that everyone has his proper place. The businessman does well to keep out of the pulpit. The clergyman or moralist very definitely gets out of his rôle when he goes into business. Even the economist, without any particularly religious sentiments, who is supposed, at least, to spend most of his time studying economic trends and making recommendations, when he is paid to do so, generally has not the time for a commercial career.

It is possible, however, that there is some common ground on which religion and business may meet and mix, apart from the rather short and casual encounter on a Sunday devotional basis. Still more, it is possible that businessmen themselves may, through their own experience, be the greatest contributors to a sound morality. While they might not consciously think of their contributions as exactly religious, they would certainly be pleased to hear that their conclusions might be good religion. They would be even more delighted to realize, the other way around, that the principles of sound religion and morality projected into business might make for greater security and better profits for all.

A short examination of the history of business shows that this is actually true. The most primitive type of commerce, still used in many parts of the world, is that of bargaining. The seller starts out by demanding an exorbitant price for his wares. The prospective buyer then has a job on his hands, not merely of getting what he wants, but also of beating the merchant down to the lowest price possible, and even of forcing him to take a loss. American tourists abroad know exactly what I mean, especially if they return home with purchases on which they have been definitely cheated. This kind of business may be interesting; but built on a system of mutual distrust, as it is, the occasional gains it may bring to one or the other party are largely offset by inefficiency and widespread losses. The introduction of fixed prices on an honest basis has been a tremendous step forward for business.

Closely connected with this type of bargaining has been what I may call the David Harum kind of deal. Readers of this famous novel will remember how clever David was in trading broken-down and wheezy horses which had been doctored up for a sale. Someone always took a loss. It is interesting to note that the word *sincere* comes from an ancient Latin expression which meant that a marble statue did not have its defects concealed with wax. The sculptors who succeeded in deceiving their patrons with this kind of trick undoubtedly profited. But the reputable merchant, who believes that a customer who returns satisfied is a better investment than a cheated customer, is careful to see that there is no wax in his wares except when specified. The standardized and honestly represented product is not only good morality; it means better business.

Take the question of labor. Labor has been and still is considered by some employers as a commodity. The idea is that a workingman should be made to give his services for the lowest possible wage. If there are many men available, then, like slaves, they should be very cheap — indeed they are to be had for any price. Reduced costs in the wages of labor should naturally make for greater profits. Farsighted businessmen, however, realize that the products of labor mean no profits at all unless there is a purchasing public to buy them. If labor is not being given a decent wage, then there is a considerably diminished purchasing public.

We may well recall the story of the farmer who bought a horse with the idea of getting the most work from the beast with the least expense to himself. He began with the ordinary rations of hay, oats, and corn. First he cut out the hay, then the corn, and began to reduce the horse's feed of oats until it amounted to one half pint a day. "Then," he complained, "just when I got the creature down to the point where she didn't need any food at all, she ups and dies." A leading American business executive recently made a statement which I think is worth wide consideration. American business, he stated, is spending millions of dollars annually to advertise its products, and failing in many instances to pay its labor wages sufficient to buy those products.

Religion, which teaches that man has an immortal soul, and therefore certain inherent rights and social duties, has been constantly pointing out that the worker is entitled to a living wage, providing, of course, he is doing a decent day's work. The experience of progressive, farsighted businessmen is to the same effect. They know that while slave wages may make some men rich quickly, nevertheless steady profits and genuine social security call for an adequate wage and the employment in industry of as many men as is reasonably possible. They call for cordial relationships between employer and employee on this basis, and for a sense of social responsibility on the part of the employer, who dominates a segment of economic life and society. This is not politics. It is good religion, and it is good business.

The same thing can be said for the field of capitalistic organization. At one time the theory that money was a commodity to be bought and sold at a profit was condemned by Catholic law. Now it is acknowledged that the changed character of industrial enterprise and the risks taken by lenders may justify a reasonable charge on money, even though its real character is that of a symbol of exchange or credit. There is still, however, a limit to which credit can be given and charged for. The tremendous transactions of today and the complexity of banking and business organizations make it easy to conceal the real nature of what sometimes goes on behind the scenes. Even the best-intentioned executives and experts often differ in what they consider sound financing. At the same time a sense of responsibility and the exercise of honesty can hardly remain a matter of sheer theory and idealism. The American public is still paying, and paying dearly, for the deals of smart but unscrupulous dealers in credits and securities, who took their fat commissions and let someone else "hold the bag."

When a counterfeiter is discovered grinding out false money and passing it into exchange, he is given a taste of the law and the indignation of all. But stocks and bonds which are issued without reasonable financial backing are equally counterfeit. A few individuals may profit on these things, but someone always takes a loss. This kind of negotiation introduced into business at large and allowed to flourish would certainly result in a collapse of all investments, and inaugurate an era of depression from which there would be no recovery. Sound business and financing realize this, and once again see eye to eye with true religion.

Of course, religion does not preach good morality simply because it means steadier profits and more social security in the long run. The Seventh Commandment was not written to make businessmen happier. As a matter of fact, this commandment and these preachments are often very annoying to individuals. Some persons are not interested in what may mean the betterment of society in the long run. They are interested only in what means bigger profits for themselves right here and now, even though the rest of business and the rest of the world collapse as a result.

But it does happen that religion teaches the law of God which fits into the scheme of the world as God sees it. And the experience of business simply bears witness to the fact that God, who has created human nature, knows what works best for it. The businessman who says that "the only thing which finally counts is what works" is right, if he means what works for the good of mankind as a whole. If he means only what works for himself or his profiting organization, and the rest of the world go hang, then he is wrong. To him religion must repeat only the words of Christ: "What doth it profit a man if he gain the whole world, and suffer the loss of his own soul?"[3] "Let no man overreach or circumvent his brother in business," says St. Paul, "because God is the avenger of these things."[4]

The trouble with many people who fail to see how religion and business can mix is that they fail to grasp the full meaning of either. Religion is not merely a matter of consoling devotion for a short period on Sunday. It is the link between man and God which runs through all life with a definite set of principles and spiritual sanctions that reach into eternity. Business is not merely the exchange of products between buyer and seller, or the accumulation of profits over costs of production. It is also a world of human relationships that involve rights and duties and social obligations as well as the freedom of personal initiative. True Christianity has always taught this, with preference for neither the employer nor the employee. In the sight of God all have their responsibilities. Business today, whether it represents capital, industry, or labor, would do well to hearken back to the Gospels, to study carefully the Encyclicals of Pope Leo XIII and Pope Pius XI, and learn that profit and progress can be placed

---

[3] Matt. 16:26.
[4] 1 Thess. 4:6.

on a solid basis only when men are willing to ask the question: "How does this square with the law of God?"

III

When people do things for us or to us, the first thing we inquire into is the motive behind the act. The gifts we receive, the favors shown to us, and the inconveniences which others put us to, all come under this relentless test, because it is precisely the spirit that has prompted the act that determines our reaction. For example, you may be standing on a crowded street corner when someone suddenly gives you a resounding thump on the shoulder. Smarting under the blow, you turn to face your assailant. If he turns out to be someone struggling with a load of bundles, you willingly accept his apology, with the explanation that the blow was entirely accidental, designed only to catch a falling parcel. Perhaps it is an old friend, who is surprised to find you in this place, and has taken this rather vigorous method of approach to gain your attention. You are glad he has gone to the pains of saluting you. On the other hand, it may turn out to be a complete stranger, who scowls when you turn to inquire the reason, and he informs you that you have crowded him out or that he does not like your face. It is quite likely that you will return the compliment in kind. If you are a woman, and the approach is made by a leering tramp who proceeds to make amorous advances, it is not improbable that you will call the nearest officer for protection.

The same truth can be brought out by a study of the accidents that happen to us. If I stumble over someone in the house, or if a jaywalker gets in the way of my automobile, I become righteously indignant, and may even threaten further action. If the object in my way happens to be a carrot, a cat, or a lamppost, my sentiments will be very different. I cannot blame the carrot, which is in no way responsible for its position, nor the cat which has very little to say about its conduct; a collision with a lamppost will make me angry with myself. At most, I can feel revengeful only with the persons who may have allowed these things to stand in their inconvenient places. If a dog bites me in the leg, I cannot sue the dog, but I may bring action against the master of the dog for permitting it to roam at large. If I bite the dog, however, its master can find redress against me.

What is true in these examples finds an eminent application in religion. Since the thing that counts in determining the value of human actions is the motive, we are quite justified in saying that what God is interested in is not so much the size or importance of the things we claim to do as the thought of divine service and love which we inject into them. A carrot and a cat are incapable of a religious act, for the simple reason that they cannot motivate anything they do with the thought of God. Compared with the forces of nature, the storm, the earthquake, the movement of celestial bodies through space of staggering dimensions, the physical acts of men seem less than microscopic. But we have within our power the motivation of our body's vegetable and animal elements and efforts under our control, and this is what imparts to them an importance which God is quick to recognize and to reward.

How many of us ever think of this? Even in acts which we call religious, how little there is of God, and how much there is of ourselves! Even while writing these lines, which are intended to convey a divine truth and to bring people closer to the thought of God, I may be moved, unless I watch myself, more by a desire of seeing my name in print than of doing something pleasing to God. The preacher in the pulpit, calling people to worship and expounding the divine mysteries, can easily fall prey to the temptation of gaining the admiration of the congregation for his eloquence and his human appeal. On his rounds through the parish, the priest may discover that he is being animated more by the hope of leaving a favorable impression and appearing a social success than of rendering a disinterested service to God. In his organization of sodalities and parochial affairs, his thrill of satisfaction in the large numbers that respond to his call and in the enthusiasm of the people for his activity may arise principally from his ambition to be successful in whatever he undertakes. He hates failure. He wants to have it said that everything he puts his hand to is worthy of commendation and of advancement. Even in his most pious functions, God may be, so to speak, a million miles away. The vegetable and the animal element in a man can easily become uppermost, unless he pauses, with calm consideration, and asks himself why he is doing these things, and attempts, by a purging of his motives to make them acceptable to God.

The same is true in every phase of divine worship. The choir in the gallery may be fairly shouting their praises of the Almighty. "*Gloria in excelsis Deo* – Glory to God in the Highest." But unless they stop, from time to time, to give thought to their action, it may become a "Glory in the Highest to Ourselves." The idea dominating every tenor and soprano may be only an exhibition of such sweet sounds as the world has never heard before, and a hope that the congregation is able to appreciate them. The difficulties of choir masters with temperamental artists are frequent enough to confirm this suspicion, particularly when disappointed soloists become quite unmanageable and overmercenary in their vocal service to God. Evidence of highly mixed motives can be found in nearly all parish societies. The organization of the Kingdom of God on earth is beset with the disconcerting problem of how to pacify rivals for offices in sodalities and conferences. There are comparatively few persons whose pure service of God can survive a lack of general appreciation. A disparaging word from the priest is often enough to ruin their religious zeal forever.

If these are practical difficulties within the inner sanctum, as it were, of God's tabernacle, we may be sure that they become truly formidable in the run of daily life where there are not the same checks and safeguards to recall this idea of purity of motive. Our tendency is to think of God only when there is some burning desire or need which He can satisfy. Danger of death, impending financial ruin, disappointment in love, desertion by friends, and the craving for fur coats and automobiles are usually infallible in provoking us to prayerful dispositions.

In the meantime, however, God figures very little in our lives. The trouble is that we are likely to regard Him as a gigantic Santa Claus who holds the strings in heaven to a bag of toys, which He could easily shower upon us, if He only would. When the prayerful urge moves us, we cry out to Him to do things for us. If our prayers are answered, we feel satisfied and complacent for the time being. If our pleas seem to be in vain, we become very resentful at His tardiness, or failure, or at the fact that the benefits He confers seem, too often, to be qualified or burdened with other conditions which take the goodness out of them. We never stop to realize that our service of Him is slow, or altogether forgotten, or so soiled with unworthy motives and considerations that it does not deserve acknowledgment.

Seldom does God demand the extraordinary and heroic from us. Our humblest actions can be made a constant offering to Him, who is our Creator, our Sustainer, our Father, and our Lover. We are continually walking in God's presence, and in some mysterious sense, everything we do is made possible by Him; else it could not come into existence. St. Paul says, "In him we live, and move, and have our being."[5] It is true that all we need, to give an act its supreme value, is a simple advertence to this fact. Yet, how few women there are who can bring themselves to realize that there is any divine romance in such humble acts as washing dishes, cleaning the house, and performing small tasks. Such, however, was the life of the Blessed Virgin. Few men pause to put into their business affairs or their handicrafts any of that communication with God which characterized the obscure labors of the carpenter Joseph and his divine foster son, Jesus.

If there were no other reason for saying one's morning prayers, they would be amply justified by the opportunity they provide for making to the Lord an offering of all the functions of the day ahead of us. And if there were no other justification for a moment's rest,

---

[5] Acts 17:28.

stolen from the routine of the day, it would be eternally valuable for a renewal of our consciousness of God's presence, of His constant support of our energies, and of our obligation to offer whatever we do, in word or in work, as a mark of our service and love for Him. The more we bring God into our work, and particularly into our routine tasks, the closer we approach the model of the ideal, Christ, who lived in constant union with the Eternal Father.

It was once a pious custom for Christians to bow their heads in a brief prayer of gratitude to God before and after meals; but we are safe in saying that comparatively few persons continue this practice. The only time many Catholics say this grace is when the priest calls for dinner, and then they say it in a confused and half-shamed fashion. There is nothing to be ashamed of in this simple but eminently intelligent and dignified recollection of God's benefits and in the renewal of our prayerful motives. If this is not Catholic action in its truest sense, we are at a loss to define it.

Besides raising our lives to a truly religious plane, the habit of motivation for God provides an excellent scale of values for distinguishing between right and wrong. While there is no natural function too ignoble to be performed as a part of God's design, it is impossible to make virtuous with a noble motive that which is evidently wrong. A person who is accustomed to offer his actions to God will have no difficulty in sensing the hypocrisy of immoral procedure, and he can find no surer test of the morality of an act than by asking himself: Is this something which I can sincerely offer as a service to God, or is there in it an element which rules out even the possibility of such consecration? One can offer to God the worthy love of friends, but he cannot offer a service of unclean thoughts and actions. God is pleased to accept the ambition of men to improve themselves culturally and socially, and to establish themselves and their families in financial competency; but no man can dare to offer to God a program of snobbery and selfishness or ask God's blessing upon enterprises of an uncharitable and dishonest nature.

These thoughts run through all Christian revelation. After relating the works of charity that should characterize a follower of Christ, St. Paul declared: "All whatsoever you do in word or in work, all things do ye in the name of the Lord Jesus Christ, giving thanks to God and the Father by him."[6] The entire life of Christ was directed by the purpose of doing the will of God, not merely in a perfect observance of the moral law, but by a consecration of all that He did in tribute and perfect obedience to His Father. Almost His last words upon the Cross were a summing up of His lifework in the words, "Father, into thy hands I commend my Spirit."[7] There can be no doubt but that on the Last Day, when we are called upon for an accounting of our deeds, God will look into our souls, not for the record of our successes and failures, but for the transforming element of all that we have done righteously – our motives.

---

[6] Col. 3:12–17.
[7] Luke 23:46.

CHAPTER 11

THE VALUE OF APPRECIATION

"Where are the nine?" (Luke 17:17).

I

THE most valuable asset in life is the power of appreciation. One of the primary aims of education is precisely to develop this power, in the sensing of comparative values. This is indeed the essence of wisdom. For it means the ability to distinguish between the wheat and the chaff, the true and the false, the genuine and the meretricious. A person who has learned to discern the beauty of nature is constantly discovering new wonders in the world of sunset, mountain, and woods, and grows great in contemplating, with the poet, the manifestations

> Of the great miracle that still goes on,
> In silence, round me – the perpetual work
> Of Thy creation, finished, yet renewed
> Forever. . . .[1]

Music, art, literature, science, history – all hold a wealth of enjoyment and personal enrichment for the individual who has learned to understand and appre-

---

[1] William Cullen Bryant, *A Forest Hymn.*

ciate them. Human nature itself becomes a fruitful study only when one has learned to recognize and to prize virtue and character. All these powers are treasures of the mind, developed slowly by experience, guidance, reading, observation, travel, meditation, and prayer; and so long as the mind continues to function, even though material fortunes disappear, they remain an abiding consolation. It has been truly said that the wise man, the man of developed appreciation, carries his wealth always with him.

If this is true, then it can be stated with equal emphasis that the most ingratiating ability in life is that of expressing appreciation. Nothing so opens up the good things of life or makes such acceptable payment for benefits received as intelligent evaluation with thanks. Nothing so effectively rings down the curtain on life's offerings as stolid stupidity in the presence of effort or refinement and the failure to express one's realization and acknowledgment of good works. The only consolation of the thoughtless, heedless person is that he may never realize what joys and riches may have been closed to him because of his intellectual or moral muteness.

No one wishes to enter into discussion with a person who is either uninterested or incapable of understanding the subject matter. No housewife cares to show her fine things, her silver and fine linens, to people for whom Wedgwood evokes the same reaction as paper picnic plates. Musicians do not like to play to audiences simply to stimulate conversation during the performance. Artists are definitely not concerned in revealing their canvases to persons of no taste or cultural understanding. Teachers hate classes that pay no attention and exhibit no desire to learn. Public speakers find it impossible to deliver their best to dull and listless audiences.

Even Christ, the meekest and most patient of men, declared to His Apostles: "Give not that which is holy to dogs. Neither cast ye your pearls before swine: lest perhaps they trample them under their feet: and turning upon you, they tear you."[2] With the same incisive language, He denounced the lack of appreciation that would be shown the messengers of His gospel: "And whosoever shall not receive you, nor hear your words: going forth out of that house or city, shake off the dust from your feet. Amen I say to you, it shall be more tolerable for the land of Sodom and Gomorrha in the day of judgment than for that city."[3] God, who has endowed man with intelligence and the power of recognition, demands an appreciation of His gifts and an unmistakable expression of thanks.

Toward God as well as man, the words of Shakespeare carry a poignant truth:

> Blow, blow, thou winter wind.
> Thou art not so unkind
> As man's ingratitude;
> Thy tooth is not so keen
> Because thou art not seen,
> Although thy breath be rude.
>
> Freeze, freeze, thou bitter sky,
> That dost not bite so nigh
> As benefits forgot:
> Though thou the waters warp,
> Thy sting is not so sharp
> As friend remember'd not.[4]

---

[2] Matt. 7:6.
[3] Matt. 10:14, 15.
[4] *As You Like It,* II, 3.

We may as well admit that thanksgiving, as the voluntary acknowledgment of goodness received, does not come naturally or easily. Children have to be taught the word *thanks* many hundreds of times before they grasp its significance and learn its appropriate use. Even then, they often feel ashamed to express their indebtedness for favors and profess a complete ignorance of what to say when the occasion of gratitude presents itself. "What do you say?" the doting parent admonishes the child who has forgotten to say thanks. "I don't remember," the child replies. "Oh yes, you do. You say 'thanks.' Now say it." "But I don't want to," the child pouts, in a mood to part with the gift rather than humiliate himself.

Youth who have had the lesson drilled into them still fail in the elemental duty of human appreciation. They frequently take what they receive in the matter-of-fact manner of a man being underpaid. The idea of reflection on the sacrifices, the planning, the eager love, and sometimes the tears that have gone into the substance of their joys on the part of others is something which they will never understand until their own turn comes to labor for their families and wonder whether all the effort and sleepless nights are worth the while.

People remember the things that they expected and failed to receive long after they have forgotten the accumulation of gifts and favors that have been heaped upon them through the years. A man will remember the failure of someone to repay a dollar, almost in the startled spirit of a frightening dream or a bad conscience, even though he has no mind to recall the many dollars that have come his way all too easily. I shall always remember, to my shame, the keen disappointment and even resentment I experienced one Christmas as a child, when Santa Claus failed to deliver the asked-for hobby horse, although Santa had found my stocking quite too small for other gifts during the many years he came down the chimney.

II

Whence comes this mean, grasping, and inarticulate spirit that chills many a friendship and puts a staying hand on many an act of contemplated generosity? Perhaps the first source is the unfortunate idea, entertained by many individuals, that everything one gets is his by right. Children, particularly the spoiled variety, feel that their parents *have* to clothe and feed them, and this becomes the *leitmotiv* or theme of all their demands. The hysteria and tantrums that accompany childish demands, until the point is won, are all the product of an inner cherished conviction that, unless every request is granted, profound injustice has been done.

Children who have never known the meaning of discipline at home are likewise a problem in lack of appreciation elsewhere. At school they assume the attitude that the teacher is being paid to put up with their insolence. They become more and more insolent and demanding as weakness is shown on the part of authorities, and more and more disdainful of what is offered them. This is the type that writes the sins of the teacher on sidewalks and fences or carves its protests against public policy on the walls of the toilets, and generally refers to schools, institutions, and other associations in terms which display at least a large lack of loyalty. Such youth, one finds, must be paid for everything they are asked to do. The scheming child who has once received a penny for doing an errand begins immediately to calculate upon an extensive business of errand running to build up a small fortune. Thereafter any form of free service becomes a distasteful imposition.

What is true in childhood becomes later welded into the character of the adult. The old adage that "the customer is always right" is a euphemism for the abuse and the insulting, inconsiderate treatment that clerks are often called upon to accept from a clientele who feel that people who receive a wage should therefore be treated like slaves and shown no mercy or appreciation. Managers and authorities, particularly of a petty category, are likewise inclined to find flaws in the work of their subordinates as an excellent occasion to reassert their power, and to pass over in silence the extra effort, the long hours, and the good work that is done, as though a word of acknowledgment and praise would be beyond the deserts of any human being.

In speaking on this subject to a group of boys, I recall asking whether it was their custom to show consideration to others, for example, by offering their seats on a streetcar to women who might be standing in the aisles. One lad quickly assured me that he had done so once, but did not feel inclined to repeat the courtesy. On my asking the reason for his reaction, he replied: "This lady leaped into my seat as soon as I arose, and she didn't even say 'thanks.' " No doubt the good woman felt she was entitled to this consideration. Unfortunately, too many of us are content to accept the gracious efforts of others in pretty much the same spirit.

The natural tendency of this outlook is to demand more and more and to give less and less in return, until even the limits of injustice have been crossed. The result is an arrogantly niggard spirit that manifests itself in a thousand ways. People who complain of the demands made upon their purse by the Church are usually the very ones who clamor for the most service, criticize every religious activity, contribute little if anything to the maintenance of their parish, and drop buttons into the religious pamphlet rack. People on public charity or relief often become exacting and domineering, finding fault with the quality of the clothing or food and threatening vengeance unless they are given *de luxe* treatment. On the other hand, successful men are frequently tempted to quit their church and forget their prayers, as though the element of divine favor were beneath contempt, and to snort at friendly requests or needs of society, as though they owed absolutely nothing to the cooperation, the labor, and the patronage of anyone. Prosperity does not necessarily lead us to a deeper insight of divine values; and many a man has been brought to a realization of his dependence upon his fellow man only when the value of the coupons on his stocks and bonds falls to the level of the paper on which they are written.

Part of this shortsightedness may be due to a hard, bargaining spirit of selfishness, which measures the whole world in terms of material profit and loss. There are persons for whom Christmas is a success or a failure, depending on whether they receive more and better gifts than they gave. Some people never give without the planned expectation of a greater return. Any bread that they cast upon the waters, they expect to return well buttered. A dinner, a book, an introduction – any favor from their hands, one may be sure, will very shortly be followed by a demand for payment as a debt of honor. This outlook, of course, engenders in the mind of scheming and demanding people the idea that everyone else is moved by corresponding motives of personal design. In the words of Vergil, "I fear the Greeks, especially when they are bringing gifts." Experience may justify this conclusion in individual instances, but to set this down as a philosophy of life is to make no allowance even for a slender margin of human kindness.

In a less obnoxious but nevertheless unfortunate form, this principle of "I give you, that you may give me" appears in the determination of people to become hard and exacting as the result of a lack of appreciation. If good deeds were to end simply because people forgot to say thanks or took what they received as their complete due, we should soon reach a sorry pass. If, for example, the boy who received no word of appreciation for his courtesy in relinquishing his seat should therefore resolve that henceforth he would refuse the courtesy, even though all the women in the world might drop in their tracks, and should adopt a similar policy for each category of kindness, as someone failed to respond, he would most certainly become nothing short of a Scrooge. The mother who teaches her child to say, "Thank you," does not end her labors of love, even though, after repeated lessons, the child is thoughtless or sulky.

Very often persons of little vision say, "Why are you doing this or that? You won't get any thanks for it." As a result of this discouragement, many a candle has been snuffed out that could have thrown its beams into a naughty world. Indeed, it sometimes requires courage to resist this type of argument. It requires an inner conviction that goodness and generosity have a real value, even though the appreciation is never expressed; and it requires patience and forbearance in the thought that much is really appreciated, although for some reason the word has not been spoken. Above all, it is the supernatural value of loving our neighbor for the love of God that makes the least act of kindness sublime.

III

The fact is that education in the art of appreciation and in its expression is a difficult one. We must not be too impatient with people who seem to be superficial or impassive in response to the good, the true, or the beautiful. The ability to evaluate is frequently purchased only by long and bitter or tedious experience. The musician whose art seems to be the product of an effortless genius has spent many years, one may be sure, toiling and suffering to perfect his technique and his power of interpretation. Such a one is in a position to appreciate great music and outstanding performance, because he knows by personal experience what obstacles must be overcome before perfection is achieved. In the same way, it is said, one never learns the value of a dollar until he has toiled to earn one and has been obliged by circumstances to stretch its purchasing power. The women who appreciate fine lace are those who have tried to make some. There is no substitute for experience in the process of achieving profound realization.

Another element in the development of appreciation is the awareness, from a personal standpoint, that every gift, every honor, every joy carries with it a corresponding responsibility. "A wise man," writes Emerson, "will extend this lesson to all parts of life, and know that it is the part of prudence to face every claimant and pay every just demand on your time, your talents, or your heart. Always pay; for, first or last, you must pay your entire debt. Persons and events may stand for a time between you and justice, but it is only a postponement. You must pay at last your own debt. If you are wise you will dread a prosperity which only loads you with more. Benefit is the end of nature. But for every benefit which you receive, a tax is levied. He is great who confers the most benefits. He is base – and that is the one base thing in the universe – to receive favors and render none. In the order of nature we cannot render benefits to those from whom we receive them, or only seldom. But the benefit we receive must be rendered again, line for line, deed for deed, cent for cent, to somebody. Beware of too much good staying in your hand. It will fast corrupt and worm worms. Pay it quickly in some sort."[5]

Shallow souls who spend their time envying the benefits which others possess or seem to possess may sometimes be excused on the score that they have no idea of the meaning of responsibility which accompanies the benefit. But those who possess the benefit and use it for its own sake, without concern for the responsibility which it entails, may well incur a similar guilt. Such has been the history of tyranny and revolution – the frivolous display and dissipation of wealth, lack of concern for the downtrodden and the poor, then the reaction of an angry discontent.

[5] Ralph Waldo Emerson, *Compensation.*

He who would aspire to the honors of high office must be prepared to shoulder its legitimate responsibilities and worries plus the abuse and the threats of cranks and agitators. Uneasy lies the head that wears a crown. He who fain would run his fingers through Midas' gold may well meditate on the thought that happiness lives in a cottage. And was it not Christ who declared, "Amen, I say to you that a rich man shall hardly enter into the kingdom of heaven. And again I say to you: It is easier for a camel to pass through the eye of a needle than for a rich man to enter into the kingdom of heaven"?[6] Fame and public repute likewise carry their burdens and annoyances, when every movement and moment in a man's life is watched by thousands and is ready to be reported by hostile as well as by friendly eyes. Beauty is no doubt a desirable gift, indeed a reflection of God's glory. Nevertheless, as exploited meretriciously or even inconsiderately, it has brought tragedy and hell to many a man and woman. Special talents hold the key to untold opportunities and good; but also, if abused or even neglected, may call for some severe accounting. "The unprofitable servant," said Christ in His parable of the man who timorously buried his talent in a napkin, "cast ye out into the exterior darkness. There shall be weeping and gnashing of teeth."[7]

Life's highways are strewn with the wreckage of the arrogant, of snobs, and of wastrels whose one ambition was to fill their own cup to overflowing even though the rest of the vintage be thrown down and lost. Such may well sing with Omar, when all is done:

---

[6] Matt. 19:23, 24.
[7] Matt. 25:30.

Indeed the Idols I have loved so long
Have done my credit in this world much wrong:
Have drown'd my Glory in a shallow Cup,
And sold my Reputation for a Song.[8]

Very frequently, in the case of all of us, lack of appreciation is due simply to a failure to sense comparative values. This defect may show itself either in a lack of vision with respect to what I actually possess and to what has gone into my gifts from God and man, or it may take the form of self-pity and of envy for what others possess or seem to possess. Both are the proof of a pygmy imagination. And the only effective way for most of us to appreciate what we have is suddenly to be deprived of it.

One never fully appreciates the joy of good eyesight until a cinder enters the eye. One appreciates the value of health only when he is stricken down and confined to a bed of pain. One never knows the meaning of peace and prosperity until he has seen the brutal devastation of war or seen poverty as the normal fare of hundreds of millions of human beings. One never fully prizes the joy of mental tranquillity until he has experienced mental suffering and fear in the worries of responsibility, the scourge of sin, or the grief of ingratitude. One can hardly appraise the gift of faith and of a sense of direction in life unless he has known something of doubt, uncertainty, and mental confusion.

It is an excellent practice for everyone occasionally to visit a hospital and see what real suffering is, to study the smile upon the face of the blind, to see for oneself the squalor of tenement districts, and to read behind the headlines of the newspapers for the

---

[8] Edward Fitzgerald, *Rubaiyat of Omar Khayyam.*

daily tragedies of rich and poor alike. It may be that suffering, even the suffering and toil of others, may help us to understand just a little bit better the value of our own humble gifts and to be thankful for what we have.

Indeed, one cannot appreciate even his own native powers until he has in some measure been tested by opposition and apparent failure. "None knows his real strength," writes Dr. R. S. Carroll, "till he has faced failure and tasted the bitterness of defeat. Physical and mental suffering and soul pain come to all that endurance may be developed, for without this the strength which conquers can never be. The master man laughs in the face of personal hurts; offenses fail to offend, insults fail to embitter; he turns with shame from the so-called depths of suffering; for him honor and majesty of soul are found upon the heights of suffering."[9]

IV

The spirit of appreciation and thankfulness is therefore one of pause and thoughtfulness, developed from a realization of obligations, responsibilities, and even of penalties. It is brought to fruition by the thought that he is most worthy of gifts who realizes the value of what he possesses, who acknowledges with humility and honor what he has received, and who puts to constructive use for the benefit of others the good that is at his disposal. Such a spirit has no time for brooding over imaginary griefs, of envying the treasures of others, or of demanding more and more for one's own personal satisfaction.

---

[9] Dr. R. S. Carroll, *The Mastery of Nervousness* (New York: Macmillan, 1917), p. 302. By permission of the author.

"The realization from a religious standpoint," in the words of Dr. James J. Walsh, "that it is better to give than to receive is one of the greatest blessings that a man can have. Nothing is so disturbing to health and happiness – and real happiness always reacts on health – as selfishness, the contradiction of the spirit of sacrifice." Nervousness may have a close relation to selfishness, and conceit, he tells us, "is the root of a great deal of unhappiness and consequent disturbance of the health of mind and body."[10] To this we may well add that the appreciative person gives quite as much as he receives, for appreciation is essentially creative, and has little time for the cultivation of conceit.

The practical art of expressing appreciation is, of course, a matter of education and long development. To be sure, some persons are instinctively thoughtful and tactful in this respect; nevertheless, a great deal can be learned by studying the amenities of cultured people and by reducing the courtesies to certain rules. We can start with the principle of taking as little as possible for granted. Our hearts may be overflowing with gratitude, but unless we make an effort to show our enthusiasm visibly, without qualifications, and to communicate our appreciation by the spoken or the written word, most of the goodness is lost.

After accepting the hospitality of others, for example, we can send a little note of thanks, a little gift, or some indication, upon our return home to show that we remember. When we receive gifts, the least we can do is to acknowledge them. When a good turn is done us, we can at least return to express our thanks. Chil-

---

[10] James J. Walsh, M.D., *Religion and Health* (Boston: Little, Brown and Co., 1920), p. 79.

dren should be taught explicitly to perform these courtesies and how to perform them. It is unfortunately true that many persons who otherwise give evidences of good breeding seem to have no developed conception of these niceties. One hardly knows whether they have received our letters, whether the gift we sent was acceptable, or whether the position we secured for them or the favor which we rendered was appreciated or not. What busy, thoughtless, selfish people we are, climbing and grasping for new friends, new acquisitions, new advancements, and forgetting even to give a nod of approval or to show that we recall what our families and old friends have given of themselves and of their stores to make life easier and brighter for us.

How few of us return, like the single healed leper to Christ, to offer our meed of thanks. And how often we find ourselves with those of whom the Master asked, "Where are the nine?"

Gratitude, as many a philosopher has noted, is the fundamental basis of social harmony. Without it, progress in civilization and culture is impossible. The blackest pages of history are those that have been written by the treachery and disloyalty of ungrateful men. And for every Judas that has crucified his dearest friend, there have been hundreds of thousands heedless small souls whose silence and neglect have been responsible for the disappointment, the tears, and the broken hearts of generous, loyal, and true helpers along the way.

In the United States, we may be proud of the fact that Thanksgiving Day is a national holiday. Every day must bring its prayer of thanks to God, after the example of Christ, whose own gratitude to His Father in heaven we can measure by his appreciation of gratitude in others: "Where are the nine?" Every single day must see some growth in the bonds of appreciation between children and parents, friend and benefactor, man and man, nation and nation. Every day must witness some new expression of gratitude for the good and the true, for the liberty, the justice, the opportunities that have been achieved for us by the men and women of the past.

Upon this basis we can build a constructive and imaginative life, one of enjoyment of true values and of preparation for eternity. We learn to appreciate every manifestation of goodness and to share that goodness with others. In the words of Emerson:

> Hast thou named all the birds without a gun,
> Loved the woodrose and left it on its stalk,
> At rich men's tables eaten bread and pulse,
> And loved so well a high behavior in man or maid,
> That thou from speech refrained,
> Nobility more nobly to repay?
> Then be my friend and teach me to be thine.[11]

---

[11] Ralph Waldo Emerson, *Forbearance.*

CHAPTER 12

RESPONSIBILITY AND CHARACTER

"No man putting his hand to the plough, and looking back, is fit for the kingdom of God" (Luke 9:62).

I

ONE of the most remarkable inner tendencies or necessities of all created life is that of fulfilling some specific task and of making some contribution to the continuity and needs of the outside world. There is, for example, an intensely interesting cycle of interdependence in the chemical exchange known as the carbon-oxygen cycle of plants and animals. The sealed aquarium illustrates the manner in which fish can furnish water plants with the materials which they need for life, while the plants supply nourishment and oxygen for the fish.

The same manifestation of an intelligent Providence is shown in the instinct of animals, not only to beget offspring, but also to provide them with food and to protect them, even at the risk of the parents' lives. In the case of animals below man, there is not involved a sense of conscious obligation, but there is a definite "pull" of nature indicating to the creature that it has a certain material accountability for acts and for effects beyond its own comfort and well-being. The hen sits on her eggs in heat and discomfort and strongly protests any effort to remove her until the nesting is done. When the chicks are hatched, she assumes a new rôle, that of picking food for her babies and of keeping them under her wing until they are ready to shift for themselves.

Raised to the level of conscious and deliberate activity in human life, this exercise of solicitude on the part of husband and wife and of parents and children constitutes the strongest and most touching factor in the continuance of the race. It is probable that few couples have an adequate conception of the responsibilities that lie before them, when they pledge their marital vows. Nevertheless, for the most part, they learn to meet the issues as they arise and to make the sacrifices that are required to justify their position as the nucleus of a family and as a unit in society. It is a fact that in the shouldering of regular obligations and duties many persons discover their true capabilities for the first time. Faced with motherhood, many a frivolous girl has become, almost over night, a generous and mature person. Stability of character and direction of purpose are revealed, often for the first time, in a young man when called upon to make a genuine and constant sacrifice of time and effort for someone and something he loves.

All in all, this sense of responsibility, extended to all departments of life, is the foundation of all greatness in character. Impulse and enthusiasm may exhibit a native generosity and may be required for outstanding achievement in various fields, but it is the steady flame of dependability based upon a trained realization that one is accountable for his acts before a higher tribunal that gives true moral value to achievement and makes predictable the outcome of human endeavor. Without this developed quality of character, the best intentions and initial movements can fall flat before the work is begun. In the words of Brutus,

> But hollow men, like horses hot at hand,
> Make gallant show and promise of their mettle;
> But when they should endure the bloody spur,
> They fall their crests, and, like deceitful jades,
> Sink in the trial. . . .[1]

It would be a serious mistake to suppose, as some educators have done, that the development of talent or the accumulation of knowledge is all that is required to bring out the best in personality. It has been demonstrated, times without number, that persons even of genius, can be extremely temperamental, unreliable, and thoroughly maladjusted to the world and to the problems they are called upon to face. The accumulation of knowledge in itself is a relative thing, both to the total of knowledge and to one's previous store of information, as well as to the equipment of others. There can be no doubt that the greater one's fund of useful knowledge and comprehension, the better prepared one should be to assume a corresponding responsibility. Nevertheless, the fact remains that the ability to assume responsibility is in large part a matter of moral courage rather than of intellectual development or vigor.

Many men of profound learning shrink from the assumption of any task which calls for executive decision or accountability. Many learned persons have shown

---

[1] William Shakespeare, *Julius Caesar,* IV, 1.

themselves incapable of managing even their own affairs, much less those of their neglected and unhappy families. So far as the education of the masses of the people is concerned, knowledge certainly means equipment for the daily requirements of the society in which we live; but it has not produced evidence of any great advance in leadership or mass enterprise. On the contrary, some of the most outstanding examples of responsible leadership in our nation and throughout history have been men of meager education and of few early cultural opportunities.

Nor should capacity for work or ambition for honor and distinction be confused with a sense of responsibility. Hard workers, particularly of an ambitious and sometimes of an invidious turn of mind, are often inclined to regard persons in places of responsibility as enjoying an easy existence, particularly if they are surrounded or protected by the symbols of distinction, and to imagine that executive and administrative offices are simply sinecures to browbeat and tyrannize over honest labor.

What they fail to realize is that honor is hardly more than the symbol of rightful authority and that there is a world of difference between the routine production of work and the business of planning that work in coordination with a social accountability. The artisan, the stenographer, or the clerk normally ends his day by the clock and goes home to enjoy his rest; but this summary attitude will not do for the man or woman whose responsibility it is to see that the organization, the investment, the general task, the commonweal is carried on and protected.

No one can have an adequate conception of what

responsibility is, or a duly respectful attitude toward it, until he has been shouldered with it. The sorcerer's apprentice, in the fable, who thought it would be great fun to cast a spell upon a broomstick and let it work for him was enormously relieved when his master reappeared and took off the spell. And many a man who has put his feet into boots that are too large for him has been only too glad to get back into his own little shoes.

Unfortunately, on the other hand, some people have such a fear of responsibility that they run from the slightest thing that appears to tie them to a task or commitment. They refuse to accept any office if it means work or worry. Their promises or engagements are always accompanied with a qualification to the effect that, if "something else turns up," they will not feel obligated to carry out the original plan. They accept the favors of others reluctantly and with the understanding that they will not be held to do anything in return. They live along the side lines of life, hesitant, cowardly, and selfish, ready to enjoy the benefits that others provide but quick to disavow any debt or obligation, the moment they are asked to contribute something in return.

Others are perfectly willing, if pressed, to go through the motions of a responsible task, but they protest that they will share none of the responsibility as such. These are the Pilates who are paid to administer justice, but who wash their hands in innocence as soon as they are called upon to face an unpleasant situation. They are the hirelings, "whose own the sheep are not" and who flee as soon as they see the wolf coming. Society cannot exist on this basis, nor can the individual work out his own redemption of character in flight or evasion.

II

Perhaps we can get a clearer idea of what the sense of responsibility is by describing what it is not. In the first place, it is not a solicitude about many things. Too many people are concerned with the affairs of others which they might better leave alone; too many like to assume the direction of affairs, or rather to go through the fussy motions of direction, in which they have no real concern, and too many load themselves with a variety of interests which simply dissipate what ability and energy they possess. In the second place, the sense of responsibility is not to be confused with the habit of worry. Worry is hardly more than a form of fear and indecision, and its strain largely incapacitates a person for shouldering responsibility. Worry is simply negative in character and futile so far as coming to grips with a problem is concerned.

The sense of responsibility is rather the realization that one has certain duties and obligations to fulfill and the determination to fulfill them to the best of one's ability. On the mental side, it involves a recognition of definite laws or principles of behavior, an understanding of the distinction between right and wrong, good and better, in detail, and an acceptance of accountability in the realm of one's free acts. On the moral side, it involves the habit of acting in accordance with these principles and of rendering oneself dependable in any set of circumstances. Fundamentally, the sense of responsibility is rooted, on the one side, in the fact that one is a free agent, endowed with a free will and capable of shaping circumstances, and, on the other, that one is answerable for his conduct to God. Responsibility has many more immediate courts to answer to, such as public opinion, one's family or dependents, and the state; but accountability to God is final, and must serve as the keystone in the formation of Christian personality.

The first step in character training, therefore, must be a training in moral principles. The desultory method of letting children pick up for themselves a code of what is right and what is wrong will not do. There must be system, using the Ten Commandments and the precepts of Christ, as the basis, with enlargement according to the development and problems of the child. The idea of sanction in the moral life, moreover, must be placed on a spiritual basis. The child must be taught that he has an obligation, not merely to avoid "getting caught," not merely to be respectable, but to make his choice of action and to answer for his conduct, in the presence of God. The regular examination of conscience and a sincere act of contrition for sin and even for imperfections of conduct should be drilled into character, as a lesson for life. In this respect of reminding the individual that he must make an eventual accounting to God, the sacrament of penance has a tremendous educational value.

The cultivation of sustained interest is one of the most difficult tasks of personal development, but is, nevertheless, one of the most important.

The power and habit of sustained responsibility can be taught by assigning certain regular chores to be done or attaching responsibility to certain forms of ownership or concession.

Children should be given regular tasks to perform, such as caring for the stove or the lawn or making their own beds, washing their dishes, keeping their rooms tidy, or something similar, so that they have the experience of suffering as a direct result of their own neglect. In this way, also, they should obtain a constructive outlook, seeing for themselves the importance and benefit, to themselves as well as to others, of fidelity to duty. Capacity for assuming responsibility successfully can be developed and increased; it can also be allowed to lie dormant or to atrophy.

I recall as a child wishing very much to own some bantam chickens. My parents finally consented to get me a pair, on the condition that I should feed and water them. My good intentions were carried out satisfactorily for a while. Then came a rude awakening, which I shall never forget, when I discovered the little rooster dying in pain, because I had forgotten to provide water for several days. The world is full of the wrecks of half-begun and half-finished projects.

Unfortunately, many people learn responsibility only through tragedy, when it is too late, or simply in the manner of a shock, which leaves no lasting positive results. How many an accident has followed from the careless leaving of toys or tools around the house, when they should have been put away. How many an "empty" gun has been fired in jest, with fatal results. How many a reckless joy rider has brought deformity or death to an innocent bystander. How often has sorrow followed upon inconsiderate drinking. What loss has been caused by the careless flicking of a match.

To a large extent, this type of harm is the product of thoughtlessness and lack of foresight. In many cases, this thoughtlessness can be identified with a lack of appreciation, total or partial, for the rightful claims which the outside world has upon the direction of our activity. A social worker in charge of the distribution of funds to the poor once told me that she never doled out relief without insisting that the applicant reserve some small mite of it as a contribution, in turn, to the church or to some public cause. No matter how poor one may be, or rushed for time, or preoccupied with great plans, there still remains some social obligation of gratitude, some moral indebtedness to society that must be taken care of.

This is a lesson which all of us can well afford to keep in mind. The easier things come our way, the less we are inclined to feel obligated to others. The children of this generation, reared in ease and comfort, provided with every advantage that science can give, and offered extraordinary educational opportunities, can visualize only with the greatest difficulty the meager physical comforts, the labors, the pains, and the sacrifices of their forebears that have made these things possible. Much can be squandered and lost by those who do not feel the responsibility of what they have been given. There is nothing more disgusting than the spectacle of selfishness and lack of vision in pampered youngsters who are bored with existence and cry out with grief and pain if they are asked to assume any responsibility that means hard work and time off from aimless play.

III

Social responsibility, of course, is a relative matter. Some people like to feel responsible for every success in a community; others are inclined to blame themselves for every failure. But there is a middle-of-the-road responsibility which corresponds to one's talents and opportunities. This is a matter of personal examination of conscience for everyone, and again we find ourselves called upon to look ahead. The student who aspires to become a priest or a teacher, a doctor, lawyer, engineer, or member of any of the professions cannot morally approach his avocation simply as the front for an easy living. Too much is involved affecting the lives, the property, the health, and the happiness of others. The doctor who attempts an operation for which he has not prepared himself may be guilty of manslaughter. The teacher who pretends competence in a subject may be answerable for fraud. The engineer or the accountant who has poorly prepared himself for his tasks can hardly be exonerated from the blame of eventual damage or loss. The priest who essays to advise his flock on important and delicate matters of conscience must be prepared to make a reckoning, if his studies in moral theology were taken lightly and with superficial attention.

There is such a thing as culpable ignorance. Mistakes are inevitable even in the course of the most careful judgment, to be sure; but the frequent reproach "he should have known better" sums up the very profound truth that there are times when ignorance is no excuse for error. There are some things which must be known and recognized and provided for. This truth has been strikingly illustrated by Christ in His description of the last judgment. Then the condemned, He said, "shall answer him, saying: Lord when did we see thee hungry or thirsty, or a stranger, or naked, or sick, or in prison, and did not minister to thee? Then he shall answer them, saying: Amen, I say to you, as long as you did it not to one of the least of these, neither did you do it to Me."[2]

The same general principle attaches to responsibility for every form of conscious activity. "I didn't mean any harm" is often a poor excuse for the evil or loss that results from an inconsiderate act. The author who puts pen to paper cannot, it is true, assume responsibility for each reaction of everyone of his readers. No one can accurately predict what some people will take out of the most simple and innocent word or statement. But the author who makes serious charges, without having substantiating proof, who stirs prejudices by misrepresentation, who excites imagination by lewd narration or description, is morally responsible, not only for the harm intended, but also for that which can be foreseen. The same is true of the spoken word, the suggestive story, the whispered calumny. A person can be intellectually and morally guilty of the sin of another even though he has had no physical part in the sin or has not even known the victim of the scandal he has given. Again, on this point Christ has spoken with vehemence, particularly against those whose bad example has deformed the character of children. "It is impossible," He declared, "that scandals should not come: but woe to him through whom they come! It were better for him that a millstone were hanged about his neck and he be cast into the sea, than that he should scandalize one of these little ones."[3]

One of the most unfortunate results of this type of

---

[2] Matt. 25:44, 45.
[3] Luke 17:1, 2.

harm is that the harm frequently persists even after the individual recognizes his responsibility and feels compunction. The story is often repeated of the woman who was seized with sorrow for her many years of spreading harmful gossip and applied to a holy man for direction on how to make amends.

"Go into the market place with a pillow full of feathers," was the advice she received. "Scatter the feathers to the four winds and come back for further instructions."

The contrite woman did as she was told and returned for advice as she had promised. "Now go about and gather those feathers back into the pillow," she was told by her sage adviser.

"Impossible," she exclaimed. "Those feathers have been scattered beyond recall."

"No more so," replied the holy man, "than the harm which you have done by an evil tongue."

The avoidance of scandal, however, requires more than a set of innocent intentions. It may be necessary to take careful stock of who and what one is with reference to the occasion and the circumstances. What may be acceptable for one person or at least relatively acceptable for one occasion may not do for another person or another time. *Noblesse oblige* says an old proverb, signifying that a person of special dignity or character must shoulder special responsibilities and conduct himself in a manner in keeping with his station.

What these times and occasions and proprieties are, everyone must study for himself. A priest is called upon to exercise extraordinary circumspection of language and conduct, avoiding many things which in others would be entirely innocent and proper. Men and women of leadership in their community cannot indulge in certain amusements or appear in certain places without compromising their influence for good and letting down the bars to various forms of license on the part of the folk who look up to them as to a stabilizing force or ideal.

There are certain formalities of dress, speech, and action, whose symbolic value is far greater than the mere mechanical gesture or aspect might indicate. One cannot disregard this fact, for reasons of personal convenience, or assume an unconventional attitude toward such things, as if they were of no account, without losing caste and thereby lowering the standards in his sphere of influence or throwing into confusion a sector of society. The society buds of every community, the beaux and belles of Hollywood and Broadway, the more or less important boys and girls, men and women in every unit, preach by their actions and attitudes a gospel of life as loudly and vehemently as any pulpit in the land. The irresponsible and "I don't care" attitude, like any other indication that the great and the near great may give to their followers, plays an important part in shaping the lives of the thousands of people; and they must answer for its consequences.

This does not mean that one should develop an ultraconservative mentality, or shrink within oneself, repressing normal and healthy impulses, weighing morosely the consequences of every little act, and hesitating to come to a decision of any importance. On the contrary, no one can really say that he has reached maturity and acquired executive ability until he has learned how to come to a decision. On occasion, this may require bold action and courage and willingness even to run the risk of error. It is perhaps too much to expect that a judge or jury should be infallible; yet a verdict must be rendered on the evidence as presented. An employer, who is called upon to hire and discharge personnel, must act with decision and finality, even though he knows he may not be liked for it. Life is full of alternatives, some involving decisions of conscience, others simply choices of advantage. One must make up his mind and act, and learn not to brood either before or after the decision has been made.

As a matter of fact, one must be careful not to confuse a morose or brooding spirit with a sense of responsibility. Some people are constantly at sixes and sevens with themselves, deeply disturbed as to whether they have committed sin or not, made due amends or not, made promises or not, treated others courteously or not, paid their bills or not, or set the alarm clock or not. Such mental instability can make a person totally incapable of assuming responsibility and may call for some careful personal direction or even medical treatment.

The spirit of responsibility, in the last analysis, is rather one of generosity, determination, and perseverance. It gives freely of its time and energy and is never spent out, because it is identified with the will to serve. In this respect, the man or woman of responsibility does not keep working hours or throw down the tools at the end of a working day. The stability and security of the enterprise with which he or she has has been entrusted is a twenty-four hour a day proposition. There is no such thing as a six-hour, five-day week for a responsible mother or father. The head of an office or bank, a professional man in any field, must give all his energies, his very life, to his work if it is to succeed.

In other words, the moral obligation of responsibility is a continuous thing, like character itself; and from this there is no vacation. A man who is honest part of the time is not an honest man. Such a person is not worthy of the trust of caring for the property of others. A man who is dependable only during the intervals when he is not drinking cannot be said to be truly dependable. A man who cannot be relied upon to keep his promises except when it suits his convenience to keep them can hardly be called reliable and cannot expect the confidence of others. People for whom the only rule of life is whim and mood will find that opportunity after opportunity passes them by. When serious issues are at stake, we are not going to place our affairs in the hands of those who tire easily, change their minds on a moment's notice, or are likely to walk off with our treasures under their arms.

It is precisely the element of constancy and sustained moral principle that makes personality a definite and tangible thing, that measures the capabilities of a person, and indicates his capacity. It is this that serves as the yardstick of friendship and love. As Emerson says:

> A ruddy drop of manly blood
> The surging sea outweighs.
> The world uncertain comes and goes,
> The lover rooted stays.[4]

In the largest degree, we can test our own possibilities for success in life by the measure in which we can bear our burdens and share those of the world about us.

[4] Ralph Waldo Emerson, *Friendship.*

Talents, advantages, energy, imagination, and all the graces of nature are but so many illusions without this ability. More than that, they may become a heavy moral burden. Speaking of the character of his great hero, Samuel Johnson, Boswell declared: "The solemn text, 'Of him to whom much is given much will be required,' seems to have been ever present in his mind, in a rigorous sense, and to have made him dissatisfied with his labors and acts of goodness, however comparatively great; so that the unavoidable consciousness of his superiority was, in that respect, a cause of disquiet."[5]

Men and women striving for perfection of personality in the manner of Christ and seeking to raise their lives above the humdrum of animal existence to a spiritual and creative conception of their powers and purpose will find much food for fruitful meditation in this abiding thought of bearing and sharing. And the stability and progress of society will be eternally in their debt.

---

[5] James Boswell, *The Life of Samuel Johnson* (New York: E. P. Dutton and Co., 1919), Everyman's Library Ed., Vol. II, p. 616.

CHAPTER 13

TRUTH AND PERSONAL INTEGRITY

"And the fire shall try every man's work, of what sort it is" (1 Cor. 3:13).

I

AMONG the famous parting injunctions to his son Laertes, old Polonius left this gem, well known to every student of literature:

> This above all: to thine own self be true,
> And it must follow, as the night the day,
> Thou canst not then be false to any man.[1]

To crack the kernel of truth in regard to oneself, however, is no easy task. "What is truth?" said Pilate to Christ; but before he could get the answer, he departed.[2]

Philosophers tell us that just as the will aims necessarily at something under the aspect of its goodness or desirability, so the mind reaches out by its very nature toward what is true. Still more profoundly, we learn that truth is the correspondence between the mind and an object outside the mind, and that the truth of things lies finally in their correspondence with the mind of God, which apprehends all things.

---

[1] William Shakespeare, *Hamlet,* I, 3. [2] John 18:38.

Students of theology go one step further and explain the distinct Personality of the divine Son as the eternal contemplation of the divine mind upon its own truth. St. John the Evangelist thus referred to Christ as the expression of God's mind or the *Word.* "In the beginning," he wrote, "was the Word: and the Word was with God: and the Word was God. . . . And the Word was made flesh and dwelt among us (and we saw his glory, the glory as it were of the only begotten of the Father), full of grace and truth."[3] In this sense also Christ referred to Himself as "the Way, the *Truth,* and the Life."[4]

Notwithstanding our divine prototype in the mind of God and the natural function of the human mind, the genuine attainment and the expression of truth frequently meet with serious obstacles. A disorderly imagination, impatience with investigation, fear, ambition, and the strange human quality known as malice, have a way of playing havoc with truth and reality. What emerges after our self-interest has finished its little task of re-creation is often very far indeed either from what we really are and think or from what really exists in the world of fact.

The creative power of the imagination is one of the most priceless possessions that we have, but it can also become one of the most dangerous. Childhood is filled with a charming world of fairies and fancies, heir of the folk lore of ages, and constantly active in games of make-believe; but make-believe can also lead to fantastic hallucinations and harmful complexes. Art, literature, music, and the drama in its various forms, not only relieve the tedium of existence, but also serve

---

[3] John 1:1–14. [4] John 14:6.

to uplift the human spirit and enrich our capacity to appreciate our spiritual nature and its relationship to God. On the other hand, they can also develop queer senses of values. The power of imagination is what leads to scientific discovery and to the enlargement of all the horizons of knowledge. But this selfsame activity, as the history of crime and war amply attest, can play strange and mischievous tricks, unless brought under careful control.

How shall we account for these strange aberrations of so noble a faculty? It must be remembered that the imagination is an organic faculty, a function of the brain, and as such is distinct from the mind or intellect, which is a spiritual faculty of the soul. Even the lower animals have something of an imagination. Dogs bark in their sleep, indicating that they have dreams. The fantastic character of many of our dreams is sufficient indication of what the imagination can do when it is not regulated by judgment or full consciousness. Extremely impressionistic, the imagination, during our waking hours may become the seat of any number of psychological complexes, such as fear or inferiority. As an organic faculty, the imagination can become disordered or warped by an injury to the brain, fatigue, or sudden shock, and lead to unbalanced thinking and even temporary or permanent insanity.

Various forms of obsession, a haunting sense of persecution, erotic images, the dread of being alone or in certain places, and frequently what are called "set ideas" are products of a disorderly, poorly trained, injured, or diseased imagination. With such an instrument, it is obvious that clear, calm, honest thinking may be seriously handicapped.

As children, we have all indulged in the luxury of a run-away imagination, particularly when, in our judgment, we were punished, unfairly or excessively. "They'll be sorry when I am gone," says the grieved child to himself meditating on running away, or, as already said, picturing himself as dead, in his little coffin, with all the guilty family shedding bitter tears for the wrong they have done. The adult mind is capable of being misled by the same type of dishonest thinking, of working itself into tremendous hates, of developing various prejudices, and taking comfort in self-pity, in flight from reality and from truthful self-examination.

In many instances, the imagination may be stimulated by deeper impulses and instincts that require considerable searching and analysis to be brought out into the light. Children occasionally cause untold mischief by retailing the most plausible lies and carrying fanciful tales from their homes to neighboring families. They seem hardly to recognize the difference between truth and falsehood. Often, there appears to be no reason whatsoever for their withholding the truth or spreading the falsehood. The same type of dishonesty carries over into adulthood. Some persons are known to be unreliable in practically every report they volunteer.

II

To make an exhaustive investigation and analysis of all the impulses and motives that underly these human quirks would carry us far beyond this chapter. Each one of us must examine his own particular problem or tendency if any practical good is to result. It may be said, however, that most dishonesty and untruth spring from some desire of self-glorification, or self-advancement, or self-protection.

The child who tells tall stories and becomes adept at the art is frequently merely looking for attention. He soon learns that unusual details attract attention; his sense of importance is flattered by listeners, particularly if they are adults. This is true in the telling of any story, by children or adults. The fish becomes longer with every telling, embellishments are added to command greater interest, and the teller shares in the dramatic importance of the event. Exaggeration thus lifts one from mediocrity; our own exploits reach heroic proportions, and we become important with the strength of our statements. It is a matter of the *ego* at work.

The same general type of intellectual dishonesty carries over into many fields. People make strong and positive statements about things on which they are very poorly equipped to speak. We are all inclined to label persons and movements and in the process to do a great deal of mischief. "Communism," "Fascism," "subversive movements," and similar epithets have been hurled about without much discrimination in recent years and often unfairly. Public speakers, particularly on graduation days or other special occasions, make sweeping generalizations about the corruption of youth, the degradation of education, and the like, which are, to say the least, inaccurate. The pulpit itself is at times guilty of bromides, clichés, and overstatements or simplifications, delivered with a vehemence in inverse proportion to the speaker's more deliberate thinking processes.

To correct this tendency requires a sincere regard

for the truth and a positive determination to be accurate. If people were to adopt this policy, it is probable that much less would be said; but the result would not be an unmixed evil. Before one spreads a story about another, he ought to ask himself whether he really has the facts of the case. Before I label someone or something, I ought to know exactly what I am talking about. Before I pass judgment on men and affairs, particularly when the good name of others is at stake or moral issues depend on my word, I ought to ask myself: "Do I really think this? Or am I simply mouthing something I have heard some place once upon a time? Am I expressing an honest conviction or is this simply a platitude to make myself appear wise? Am I qualified to discourse, or teach, or advise as I presume to do?" Honest speaking, like honest thinking, may call for much self-discipline.

Some persons never speak what is on their mind. If the tendency is merely to make pious remarks with no substance behind them, to engage in a type of sparring persiflage, or even to praise excessively, no harm need come of it. We simply recognize the evidences of a superficial mind in such activity, and we learn to discount most of the sentiments expressed. The same is true of the thin veneer of what is popularly called "bluff" – that sort of bluster and brass in speech and action, by which some "make the most" of what they have and inject themselves into positions of importance or attention for which they are poorly equipped.

But when there is question of a cunning and scheming mentality, there is an altogether different problem. This type of mind never comes out into the open. The cards are never laid on the table. One never knows what to trust and what to suspect. Hidden motives are behind every move. Intrigue and double dealing are the substance of all activity. There is question here, not merely of a two-faced policy, but of as many faces as there are persons to be dealt with. To one person, it is one story; to another person, it is another.

Literature is full of malicious double dealing and the sorry ends that it has brought — Shakespeare's Iago, Dickens' Uriah Heap, Congreve's Maskwell, and a thousand others. History tells the same sordid story, and life brings similar experiences to us all. One might almost think that some individuals are born with crooked minds, incapable of thinking along straight and honest lines and of expressing themselves openly and sincerely.

Not all double dealing, however, is the product of direct or conscious malice. A good deal of it proceeds indirectly and sometimes almost innocently from some form of personal weakness. A weak administrator, for example, instead of facing his organization as a whole and proceeding to co-ordinate its various branches, may insensibly find himself resorting to the expedient of seeing everyone privately and, as it were, toadying to each with a different story or set of concessions, thus building up a tissue of misunderstandings and divisions. Instead of facing an uncomfortable situation squarely, such men are inclined to agree with everyone in turn and consent to fix the blame on each successively. This, of course, postpones the day of reckoning; but it does not solve the problem permanently.

Envy and jealousy likewise give rise to much devious

reasoning. Instead of reaching our secret impulses and bringing them squarely to task, we begin calling things by different names, praising excessively here, and intriguing just as vigorously there, until we have succeeded in attaining our object or have ended by revealing ourselves for what we really are. As a result, the lives of many people are strewn with broken promises, lost friendships, evasions, and distrust. For such, there is no clear distinction between "yes" and "no," no clarity of decision, no courage of conviction, no finality of will. Complacency thus becomes a form of cowardice, apparent agreement only a kind of temporizing, and kindness, merely stealth.

III

The solution of these problems must begin with the courage and determination to face the truth about oneself. There must be a willingness to acknowledge one's own shortcomings, failures, and guilt for what they are, not rationalizing or finding comfort in what we may call good reasons for bad conduct, or pitying oneself for the accumulation of circumstances which call for accounting. *Gnothi Sauton,* says the ancient Greek adage — "know thyself." If we are to present to the world an integrated and positive personality, we must begin by insisting upon a transparency of soul within ourselves.

This does not mean that we are to become introverts to the point of questioning our honesty of motive in every act or decision; nor is honesty of purpose any guarantee that the world will give us credit at all times for the desire of doing what is right. What others may think is not of primary importance. Nevertheless, the Christian practice of a daily examination of conscience is of the utmost importance, beginning with a prayer to the Holy Spirit for divine guidance, then a study of our actions and policies in the light of our underlying purposes and of our constant weaknesses and inclinations. We can then fittingly end with an act of sorrow for what was wrong and a prayer for God's help in the future.

Such a study may not seldom reveal that we have been governed by certain principles or standards drilled into us or adopted by assimilation during formative or "hardening" periods. It has been an interesting experience for me, as for everyone, to meet schoolmates some time after they have left school and witness the change of character and outlooks that has taken place under new circumstances and under new mentors. Some carry on steadfastly as they began – "the same old John," we say, or "the same Anne." Others change, sometimes radically. What they once thought or believed now seems stale. They have adopted new gods, new evaluations, reflecting what their new associates or guides think about life. It is easy for a person to have one set of original basic and formal principles and at the same time to acquire a set of "practical" applications or modifications that do not hang well together.

I remember on one occasion, after delivering a lecture on civic honesty, the reaction of an old lady who, although a pious soul, I am sure, was reared in a familiar school of practical politics. "I've always been taught," she said, "and I still maintain that 'God helps them that help themselves.'" The evolution of honesty and truth from simple, elementary principles, into complex and vague systems hinging on personal convenience or group acceptances is indeed interesting and is often so gradual that even the individual himself is unaware of the change that has taken place or of the complete inconsistency of his inner piety with his outward practice.

A personal sense of honesty rigorously adjusted to high and inflexible standards is necessary, if one's good intentions are to survive the numerous and subtle tests that crowd into every life; and training in this sense of principle cannot begin at too early an age. I may be permitted to recall that someone presented me, when a very small boy, with two pennies, one for myself and another for my younger sister. As children will do, I put one of the pennies in my mouth and in a moment swallowed it. As soon as realization of the awful truth dawned upon me, I rushed to my mother with news of the tragedy, hastening to add that it was my sister's penny that I had swallowed. Actually, I cannot remember whether I honestly thought this or whether I made up my mind from perverse selfishness. I do remember, however, I was made to understand that I had assumed an obligation in accepting the gift; and the remaining penny went to my sister. The lesson was a good one.

My first recollection of a dishonest act was the theft of some flowers from a neighbor's garden. I admired the flowers, and an older boy advised me to pick them. It seemed proper to ask permission, but as no one was there, my friend suggested that I should not be discovered and that in any event no great harm would be done. When I brought the flowers home and explained how I had secured them, I was given my first lesson as to the meaning of others' property and was administered a silent treatment for the rest of the day. Somehow, I shall never forget this incident.

Another childish impression which has never left me was that produced by my hearing that a certain gentleman, the president of a local bank, had been seen to destroy his railroad ticket when the conductor failed to take it up. It seemed to me at the time that the bank was in very safe hands, particularly when many people declared that they would have kept the ticket and used it again.

The reason I mention these incidents is simply to stress the importance of early impressions and lessons. Many parents boast in the presence of their children of having short changed someone and make it clear that they feel no compunction in certain forms of dishonesty. Childish pranks involving theft from neighboring gardens or stores and destruction of property are often regarded with indifference or laughed off as great fun by elders who should know better. Sometimes children are encouraged or even ordered by their parents to perform certain chores clearly involving fraud or larceny.

The transition from a childhood of loose conceptions to a youth in which cheating and theft are regarded as legitimate forms of competition, and thence to maturity sanctioning an "enlightened self-interest" which means the law of the jungle, is quite natural and organic. There is no point in examining a conscience that has been hardened in modes of thought and standards of action to deny any difference between right and wrong in matters of personal concern.

The question of personal integrity goes even deeper than the distinction between right and wrong, truth and falsehood, honesty and dishonesty. It is rooted in a sense of the values of life itself. If, for example, a person starts out with the assumption that the most important thing in life is money and the acquisition of money, he can sell out his friends, his position, his usefulness, and his very soul for money and yet apparently not allow himself, externally at least, to be disturbed by the heinousness of his act of dishonesty. Many a man has abandoned the conception of a life purpose, the clear indications of personal talents, and has come to despise action of an idealistic character, simply because the inducement of a few extra dollars in another position or field has led him to "improve his condition." One of the great temptations in life is to place a monetary value on every act and to regard as wasted the moment that does not produce cash. The world is full of people who are telling their cozy consciences the lie that an opportunity for material gain cannot wait for a decision as to whether that gain is worth a spiritual loss or whether it involves considerations of a moral nature.

IV

Perhaps, in the course of this study, someone may ask why truth and honesty are considered under the same heading of personal integrity. In some respects, their competence is in totally different fields. Nevertheless, from a personal standpoint, the two are constantly joined, in the spirit of disinterestedness and courageous conviction. The saints have been men and women who scorned personal gain in the goods of the world, when this meant superfluity for their needs or taint of quality and motive, and they have clung to the truth in the same passionate desire for unity with God, even though their determination cost them persecution and death. Christ, the unblemished leader, declared that the birds of the air have their nests and the animals their holes, while He did not have whereon to lay His head.[5] Because He was no respecter of men, so far as truth was concerned, He was led to the death of the cross. Yet to Him, because of this sheer disinterestedness, we owe the supreme blessings of our existence and the hope of an eternal life.

One must never allow himself to lose faith in these principles. There is so much deceit and dishonesty in the world, so much unscrupulous propaganda, so many forms of circumvention, that one might come to the conclusion that the whole social fabric is a fraud and that the only way of living is to adopt the same crooked means that are employed by others. Even from a material standpoint, however, falsehood is eventually exposed for what it is. The struggle for truth, no matter how painful and confusing at times, still remains the proper function of the human mind. Christ's Beatitude declares: "Blessed are they that hunger and thirst after justice, for they shall have their fill."[6]

In the words of the poet:

> Truth, crushed to earth, shall rise again;
> The eternal years of God are hers;
> But Error, wounded, writhes in pain,
> And dies among his worshippers.
>
> Yea, though thou lie upon the dust,
> When those who helped thee flee in fear,
> Die full of hope and manly trust,
> Like those who fell in battle here.

---

[5] Matt. 8:20.
[6] Matt. 5:6.

Another hand thy sword shall wield,
Another hand the standard wave,
Till from the trumpet's mouth is pealed
The blast of triumph o'er thy grave.[7]

This does not mean that one should necessarily assume the air of the martyr for truth or stubbornly insist that he have the last voice in every argument. Truth does not function that way. Rather, the sane attitude is one of honest and patient enquiry for the truth, a desire to adequate the facts so far as possible, a clean-cut and natural determination that nothing but the truth and honest dealing will do. To assume that one is always right, that there is nothing further to be learned or said, that those who differ are therefore in the wrong, is not the pathway to truth but the expression of a small and conceited mind.

The history of mankind reveals that what has been done of a constructive, progressive, upward nature has been the result of an earnest search for the truth and a determination for honest dealing. Science and what there is of value in literature and art are the disinterested expression of truth in some form or the other. Religion itself can survive only in those elements which are authentic and correspond to the rational aspirations of mankind on the one hand and to divine revelation on the other. The rest must fall by its own weight, no matter how seriously it is taken by an age or a generation that has lived under the blanket of deceit.

The same is true of every individual. What is true, genuine, and sincere remains to the credit of the human personality. What is false and meretricious,

---

[7] William Cullen Bryant, *The Battlefield.*

sham, pretense and dishonesty, simply works toward disintegration and is eventually exposed. The line of development for Christian personality and personal integrity is clear. The human mind can find no rest or reconciliation except in the habit of constitutional candor with itself. Not until this has been achieved is one authorized to pass judgment on the world.

The Pharisees who sought to ensnare Christ gave their case away when they acknowledged His superiority with the words: "Master, we know that thou art a true speaker and teachest the way of God in *Truth.* Neither carest thou for any man: for thou dost not regard the person of men. Tell us therefore what dost thou think?"[8] Christ's answer on that occasion and on every similar occasion points the way to character and strength.

In the last analysis, personal integrity means more than self-respect and far more than mere apprehension of what consequences may be. It is built essentially upon a spirit of disinterestedness. It asks only what is right and just: it seeks to give true value for value; it is concerned only in what may prosper the worthy cause, the common good. The man who is at one with himself is, by the same token, a benefactor of mankind, a genuine force for progress, a light in the confusion of darkness, and a pillar of strength to all that waver in darkness and yet would see the light.

---

[8] Matt. 22:16–17.

Chapter 14

THE MINISTRY OF BEAUTY

"With thy comeliness and beauty set out: proceed prosperously, and reign" (Ps. 44:5).

I

DESPITE all that practical men may say about the prime importance of making a living, of keeping body and soul together, of devoting one's first efforts to the material considerations of life, there can be no doubt that there is another quest in life, one of equal, and in many ways of greater, importance — the quest of beauty. No matter how humble the cottage, there must be at least some potted flower in its window or in its yard. No matter how bare the room, there must be some picture on the wall and a window to let in the beauty of the sun and the stars.

The recognition of beauty, however noble or depraved it may be, is indeed one of the first signs of intelligence. Animals can perceive objects and tell instinctively which are good for them and which may be harmful. But the resplendence of form and proportion is reserved to man, who can appreciate the relations of parts to the whole and see in such arrangement the activity of a superior mind. Dogs bark at the moon and are distressed by music. In the presence of a sublime sunset or of the canvas of a master painter, they remain unmoved, except in so far as their sense of sight is affected. But in the souls of men there stirs a distinct reaction. The aesthetic sense, as it is called, produces through the reasoning faculties a joy that rises above considerations of usefulness or harm, dimensions, odor, sound, color, or material satisfaction.

For many men the quest of beauty has been so exclusive that they have rooted their happiness in its momentary attainment. According to Walter Pater, "a counted number of pulses only is given to us of a variegated, dramatic life. How," he asks, "may we see in them all that is to be seen in them by the finest senses? How shall we pass most swiftly from point to point, and be present always at the focus where the greatest number of vital forces unite in their purest energy?"[1]

This, of course, represents the very refinement of artistic search and is indeed hardly more than a feverish escape from most of life's realities. Even to select the beautiful elements means something of a laborious search with much painstaking selection from a mass of mediocre and frequently hideous items. Nevertheless, the search and the selection are worth the while. Life without beauty in it and personality without the conscious experience and thrill of the beautiful are indeed lacking in an essential factor of happiness.

Where shall we look for this element of vital beauty? What constitutes a legitimate and satisfying object of appreciation? There ought to be some standard of

[1] Walter Pater, *The Renaissance* (New York: Macmillan, 1906), pp. 249–250.

values, some basis of judgment, so that our energies will not be wasted in the pursuit of vanishing pleasure or tragic delusion.

Heinrich Heine maintained that the pleasure of beauty is to be realized through sensual experience in the wide sense. "The fairer and happier generations that will rise up and bloom in the atmosphere of pleasure," he wrote, "will smile sadly when they think of their poor ancestors, whose life was passed in melancholy abstinence from the joys of this beautiful earth, and who faded away into spectres from the mortal compression which they put upon the warm and glowing emotions of sense."[2]

It is true that we are free to grant ourselves the rational enjoyment of the senses. Sight, sound, taste, touch, and odor, it may be added, can contribute to heighten aesthetic pleasure and often, by their harmony, are its source. The saints no less used these to heighten their love of God. But whether the enjoyment of the emotions of sense is on a physical level or on higher planes of intellectual appreciation, it seems clear that the Creator has intended that they should serve the purpose of a useful impulse and immediate reward in performance of a natural function. To deny this is to deny the very nature of man and to fall into the error of the ancient Manichaeans, who thought that the entire material world was the work of the devil.

On the other hand, mere indulgence of the senses can lead to anything but nobility and beauty. As John Ruskin observed, "It will be found with all the senses, that they individually receive the greatest and purest

[2] Cf. Matthew, Arnold, *Essays in Criticism,* first series (New York: Macmillan, 1895), p. 216.

pleasure when they are in right condition and degree of subordination to all the rest; and that by the over-cultivation of any one (for morbid sources of pleasure and correspondent temptations to irrational indulgence confessedly are attached to all), we shall add more to their power as instruments of punishment than of pleasure."[3]

No less than this Heine himself was obliged to confess as he lay on his deathbed, wracked with pain and totally disillusioned by the fragile framework of nerves and senses. Unfortunately, many people never come to this realization. Their lives being stuffed with distractions and their consuming ambition, a bourgeoisie desire of physical comfort and convenience, they never rise to a higher appreciation of the beauty that lies around them, not only in the harmony of material elements and in artistic creation, but also in the world of spiritual relationships.

For those who can rise above the desire for mere sensual gratification, suffering itself, endowed with noble motive or moral purpose, assumes true grandeur and beauty. The lines of sorrow on a mother's face, the protest against oppression painted in Millet's masterpiece, "The Man with the Hoe," the sufferings of Christ, and the figure of His anguished body stilled in death upon the Cross, are sublime examples of a beauty far greater in conception than "the atmosphere of pleasure" described by the young Heine. Suffering, privation, and sacrifice are by no means the brutish thing that pagan minds represent them to be. The blood that ran down the wood of the Cross has transformed that symbol of suffering into a mighty tree with mag-

---

[3] John Ruskin, *Modern Painters,* I, part 3, *Of Ideas of Beauty.*

nificent foliage and richest fruit, and taught us the universality of a spiritual beauty available to all men.

Some have found in beauty and the fine arts a refuge from the harsh realities of life. It was thus that Oscar Wilde declared himself in the thought: "It is through Art, and through Art alone, that we realize our perfection: through Art, and through Art alone, that we can shield ourselves from the sordid perils of actual existence."[4]

This sentiment represents something of the cynical pose of a decadent, although philosophers of pessimism like Schopenhauer have seriously cried out for music and art to come to their rescue in a cruel world. The fact is, however, that the expression and appreciation of beauty and art in its various forms does serve, not necessarily as an escape from existence, but rather as an inner need of the human spirit. There is something essentially creative in art, inasmuch as it requires deft and harmonious arrangement and, by its symbolic nature, conveys a spiritual meaning beyond the arrangement of line, color, sound, or rhythm. This inner need and creative impulse exists in all people as a special form of intelligence, greater in some persons than in others, more developed in some nations and epochs than in others, assuming at times the character at once of a genius and a hunger quite out of proportion to other elements; and, it may be added, religion, particularly the Catholic religion, has fostered and stimulated this impulse and gratified this need.

Thus travelers in Catholic countries are frequently amazed at the wealth of beauty and art expressed in

[4] Oscar Wilde, *Intentions* (*The Critic as Artist*) (New York: Doubleday, Page and Co., 1923), p. 185.

churches and other religious monuments, often side by side with the humble dwellings of the poor. For example, the question is often asked why there are so many churches in Mexico. There are many answers to be given; but the most direct and simple answer, it seems to me, is that the people like to build them. Perhaps, from a material standpoint, they might do better to spend their effort and substance on improving their own homes. The fact is, nevertheless, their highest energies are put forth in a community effort. They rise to their greatest in the expression of enduring beauty, and it can hardly be held to their discredit that this beauty is consecrated to God.

II

To suppose that a person of high artistic talent or appreciation must therefore be a person of great virtue is, of course, as false as to suppose that a superior scientist or good mechanic is necessarily also a good man. Many artists have been bad morally and maladjusted to the life about them. On the other hand, it can hardly be doubted that the appreciation of fine art in any form is essentially ennobling in itself. One of the essential functions of education, whether formal or self-directed, should be the development of a taste for the higher and finer things in art, music, and literature.

Precisely in the emotional appeal of art lies its subtle power for the elevation of the mind and the toning of the general culture. Because beauty appeals to the imagination, it is a facile vehicle for the presentation of truth; and because it arouses the emotions, it is a ready stimulant to action.

The mental life may be divided into the life of intellect and logic and the life of emotion and sympathy. The second follows from the first, but considered from a practical standpoint, it is the more potent of the two. For, judiciously exercised and economized, nervous energy propagates itself back into mental activity. Thus it gives to the intellect a facility of conceiving things from the standpoint of personal interest and imparts to concepts the vigor of imagination. Our appreciation of situations, our grasp of ideas, our mental alertness and outlook on life in general are broadened and deepened; our capacity for happiness and usefulness is increased.

Beauty, in a word, is the imaginative expression of an underlying idea, and aesthetic appreciation is reflected in the emotional apprehension of this idea. Granting the influence that emotions exercise upon our lives and personalities, we must learn to love only true and wholesome beauty and to encourage others to form this orthodox and higher taste. For the emotional aspect of an idea gives it moral color; and the aesthetic, born of this emotional aspect, conveys it more subtly than any reasoned process can hope for.

Beauty thus becomes a significant element, not only in the realm of the intellect, but indirectly in the moral realm of the will. Development of the powers of aesthetic discrimination becomes a positive duty for those especially who are placed over the direction of souls; and it is for all an educational process hardly to be equaled in cultural value. In recognizing and dwelling with the beautiful, we are elevated into the regions of higher thought and imagination. And inasmuch as created beauty is a symbol and model of the Ideal Archetype, we may truly be said to be brought closer to God Himself.

The idea that humanism and Christianity cannot be reconciled is based on a false view of both. For Christianity aims to take all that is good in life and impart to it a spiritual value. It does not alter true humanism, but places it in the service of God. What was formerly a naturalistic perfection it endows with a higher significance.

Some poets and tasters of the exquisite in life have asserted that beauty need look for none of these purposes to justify its place in the rational world. So wrote Emerson in his famous lines on the flower:

> Rhodora! if the sages ask thee why
> This charm is wasted on the earth and sky,
> Tell them, dear, that if eyes were made for seeing,
> Then beauty is its own excuse for being.[5]

Keats approached this thought in a passage perhaps more striking than critical:

> "Beauty is truth, truth beauty," – that is all
> Ye know on earth, and all ye need to know.[6]

The more one studies this question, the more one realizes, however, that truth and beauty are, under certain respects, in the same category. Just as truth rises above individual facts and hearkens back to some supreme norm or standard of comparison, beauty soars above the material aspects of things and carries its reference to some supreme type or source of perfection. Indeed, beauty is by no means confined to the arrangement of line and color, in the physical order of the

[5] *The Rhodora.*
[6] *Ode on a Grecian Urn.*

senses, but exists also in the intellectual and moral orders.

There is genuine beauty for the mathematician in the harmony and equation of numbers. For the logician, there is beauty in the process of orderly thought. The beauty of literature lies in both the refined character of the author's conception and the aptness of his expression. Similarly we speak of a beautiful personality. Courage, honesty, purity, fidelity, kindness, and reverence represent the most perfect forms of natural beauty, and these in turn indicate an infinite perfection to which they aspire.

III

It is in the moral order that beauty finds its very highest expression, and to this order all lesser beauty directs itself. "O how beautiful," says the Book of Wisdom, "is the chaste generation with glory, for the memory thereof is immortal: because it is known both with God and men."[7] Of those who work for the peace of mankind, Isaias declares: "How beautiful upon the mountains are the feet of him that bringeth good tidings, and that preacheth peace; of him that showeth forth good, that preacheth salvation, that saith to Sion: 'Thy God shall reign!' "[8] Speaking of Wisdom, the Book of Proverbs states: "Her ways are beautiful ways: and all her paths are peaceable."[9]

The poets of nature have grasped this truth. They have seen in the rose and the daffodil not merely a passing or an accidental joy but the hand of a Master Artist and the plan of an Almighty Providence. Christ declared: "Behold the lilies of the field, how they grow:

---

[7] Wisd. 4:1. [8] Isa. 52:7. [9] Prov. 3:17.

they labor not, neither do they spin. But I say to you, not even Solomon in all his glory was clothed like one of these. And if the grass of the field, which is today and tomorrow is cast into the oven, God doth so clothe: how much more you, O ye of little faith?"[10] The beauties of nature, as Divine Scripture repeatedly points out, are intended as a constant reminder of the beauty and intelligence of the Creator. "The heavens show forth the glory of God," writes the Psalmist, "and the firmament declareth the glory of his hands. Day to day uttereth speech: and night to night showeth knowledge."[11]

The saints have been men and women profoundly imbued with this realization, rising from the joyous charm and magnificence of the beauty of the world to a deeper understanding and love for its Maker. St. Paul makes it clear that, from the fact of creation and the intelligence manifested in its order, the existence of God must be deduced inevitably. Reproaching the ancient Gentiles for their infidelity, he asserts: "For the invisible things of Him from the creation of the world are clearly seen, being understood by the things that are made. His eternal power also and divinity: so that they are inexcusable. . . . We understand that the world was framed by the word of God: that from invisible things visible things might be made."[12]

This was the constant theme in the preaching and poetry of St. Francis of Assisi. The stories which are told of his discourses to the birds and animals may be a mixture of legend and fact, but they demonstrate at least this: that the little poor man, as he called himself, constantly lived in the presence of God, for he

[10] Luke 12:27, 28. [11] Ps. 18:2, 3. [12] Rom. 1:20; Hebr. 11:3.

saw the divine perfections everywhere reflected in the beauty of the world. For him "Brother Sun" and "Sister Water" were not poetic expressions or declarations of belief in the divinity of natural forces, but rather fellow creatures with which he might join in offering glory to the God who had created beauty after "His own image and likeness."

In his *Canticle of the Creatures,* he sings:

> Praised be Thou, my Lord, with all Thy creatures,
> Especially Sir Brother Sun, Who bringeth days, and
> Thou givest light through Him:
> For he is beautiful and radiant with great splendor:
> From Thee, Most High, he gains significance.

"What a fulness of delight," writes Matthew Arnold, "does St. Francis manage to draw from this material world itself, and from the commonest and most universally enjoyed elements — sun, air, earth, water, plants! His hymn expresses a far more cordial sense of happiness, even in the material world, than the hymn of Theocritus. It is this which has made the fortune of Christianity — its gladness, not its sorrow: not its assigning the spiritual world to Christ, and the material world to the devil, but its drawing from the spiritual world a source of joy so abundant that it ran over upon the material world and transfigured it."[13]

Yet Arnold has missed an important part of the truth. For Christianity sees beauty in sorrow and suffering as well as in joy and comfort and prosperity. The most beautiful moment in the life of Christ was that of His crucifixion, not for the sordid cruelty of His death, nor the extreme poverty, as such, in which He died, but in that spirit of complete reconciliation with

[13] Matthew Arnold, *op. cit.,* p. 220.

the Divine Will to which He gave Himself, and in that perfect sacrifice of love with which He offered Himself for the redemption of mankind. The body of Christ is beautiful, not because of the blood that streams from His wounds, but because it is the supreme offering of the God-man who has been willing to "lay down His life for His friend." The heart of Christ, even in representation, is beautiful, not because of the configuration of its veins and tissues, but because it is the symbol of the love of God, who "emptied himself," as St. Paul writes, "taking the form of a servant, being made in the likeness of men, and in habit found as man."[14]

In its love for the beautiful as a reflection of the supreme beauty of God manifested in Christ, Catholic Christianity has not hesitated to offer its best talent in the social expression of art, even with a prodigality at times like that of Mary Magdalene, who poured her precious ointment upon the feet of the Redeemer, while her critics commented on "this waste." There have been times, no doubt, when human vanity has masked itself under the form of offerings to God, and instances in which the indiscretion of one age or the faithlessness of another has confused the symbol for substance. But underlying all these expressions, there must come to the man of sincere faith a richer understanding of:

> That Light whose smile kindles the Universe,
> That Beauty in which all things work and move.
> That Benediction which the eclipsing Curse
> Of birth can quench not, that sustaining Love. . . .[15]

Whether through nature or art, the beauty of the world looks inward and upward, from line and color

[14] Philip. 2:7.
[15] Percy Bysshe Shelley, *Adonais.*

and sound, to a moral sounding of the universe, and to God, whose guiding Providence notes even the sparrow's fall. Without this meaning and inspiration of created charm, we may find ourselves lamenting with St. Augustine. "Too late came I to love Thee, O Thou Beauty, both so ancient and so fresh, yea too late came I to love Thee, And behold Thou wert within me, and I out of myself."[16]

But with this union with God through the beauty of His handiwork, completed in the order of divine grace, come the words of the saint as the fulfillment of man's highest powers: "I have tasted Thee, and now do hunger and thirst after Thee: Thou didst touch me, and I even burn again to enjoy Thy peace."[17]

---

[16] *St. Augustine's Confessions,* Book X, Chap. 27.
[17] *Ibid.*

CHAPTER 15

THE MASTERY OF LIFE

"For power is made perfect in infirmity" (2 Cor. 12:9).

I

IT HAS been one of the unanswerable questions asked by the sages of the world whether the majority of men, given a preview of existence in this life, would really care to be born, aside from what a future life might hold for them. Life is thrust upon us. We are provided with the instinct of holding on to it and of expanding our powers. From that beginning, however, everyone must enter on a struggle to master his life and to find for himself an agreeable place in the world which is not particularly adapted to give a welcome.

The business of making a living, of maintaining one's position securely, and of investing the fruits of one's labors safely against changes in fortune, commands the attention of every individual. Then there is the problem of finding friends in whom one can confide and trust. Still more difficult, in many cases, is the task of preserving health of body, without which the other gifts of life are material delusions. All these elements brought under control, there remains the supreme work of shaping one's character, of calming one's temperamental difficulties, attaining poise and self-control, and governing the appetites of the flesh that drag one down from the heights of reason and self-respect to stultify and destroy oneself and one's fellow men.

Is there any secret way by which we can escape the practical certainty of life's disappointments and arrive at its bounties? Can it be that perhaps the difficulties of life are sheerly imaginary and that by some mental readjustment we can sweep away the host of physical and moral ills that torment us? There is a school of thought that regards the world merely as the projection of a dream. We are told that a person can master and mold the universe to suit himself if he but wills to do so.

It is true, I think, that some of our troubles are imaginary and that we have an exaggerated idea of many that are real. Mental readjustment can remove these to a certain extent. But it cannot restore the dead child to its grieving mother, give back fortune to the bankrupt, or undo the facts of injustice and sin. Christ reminds us that a man cannot, merely by taking thought, increase his stature so much as by one cubit. If life is to be mastered, it will be by the recognition of reality and real difficulties, and not by so simple a plan as mental suggestion or adjustment.

Against this cheerless optimism there arises the more dismal answer of resentment with life and mere compassion for those who suffer. It is easy, under the strain of misfortune, to adopt the attitude that all is disorder and confusion. The death of the young, the useful, and the virtuous is hard to accept in view of the lingering existence of the mentally defective and the hardened criminal. Prosperity for the wicked, good luck for the lazy and incompetent are hard to understand when those of clean, honest, and active lives are visited with endless trouble. Why does God permit an era of progress and growth only to be wiped out by a sudden calamity: depression, earthquake, plague, or war?

These are questions to bewilder even the steadiest and most thoughtful of men. A storm on the lake of Genesareth was enough to shake the confidence of the Apostles, even though Christ was in the boat with them. The spectacle of His arrest by the soldiers after the betrayal of Judas resulted in their complete desertion of Him, even though they had spent three intimate years with Him in preparation for this crisis. If there is a tendency toward disbelief in God today, it is not so much from intellectual arguments as from the inability of people to reconcile the mishaps and hard deals of life with the Providence that one might expect from a good and powerful Creator.

These were the difficulties of men in ancient times, and they are the source of material for doubters and the enemies of religion today. If we are to rise from this fear of life, they say, it must be by our own efforts, in defiance of the Being that men call God. When these efforts fail, we can only pity the unfortunate and bemoan the fate that brought them into existence.

They are indeed reckless blind spirits who try to stand upon their own decisions without the aid or sanction of God. They look for no life, reward, or readjustment beyond the grave. For them, human life is but the breath of the mysterious vital forces that move in the plants and animals about us. Death comes, and with it — annihilation. Of these leaders working in the darkness of night without hope, Christ once more says: "Let them alone: they are blind and leaders of the blind. And if the blind lead the blind, both fall into the pit."[1]

Far from determining the basis of noble living, they fail to assign to life the purpose it must surely have and to explain the enduring impulses of the human spirit toward immortality. Men may claim the right to make and adjust the moral law according to their liking, but there remains in everyone the deep conviction that the promptings of conscience represent something prior to the individual, framed for him by a higher Being, to accept gratefully and obey. We may be distressed by the sufferings and uncertainties of this world, but at the same time, we are impelled to conclude that behind its beauty, order, and goodness there must be a great and good Designer whose plans are well ordered even though but partially revealed.

These considerations lead even further. The more we study the history of mankind in general and of our own lives in particular, the more it is borne in upon us that toil, hardship, and disappointment are not merely elements of a universal disorder but vital parts in the plan of the Almighty to develop our energies to their highest powers. Even in this life we are afforded an occasional glimpse of the fact that apparent blessings can be a delusion and that the very things we once regarded with bitter resentment can turn out for the best.

When the Apostles sought to learn what place they would occupy in Christ's kingdom, as they understood it, Christ answered by saying: "Can you drink the

[1] Matt. 10:14.

chalice that I shall drink?" referring, of course, to the suffering and death He was about to undergo.[2] This is the test of responsibility upon which enduring rewards will be assigned. It is a fact that the finest things in life — unselfish service, charity, and sacrifice — correspond in this world not to the fulfillment of perfect working conditions and high material standards of living but to the existence of definite obstacles, of needs, reverses, and tragedies.

The true heroes, those whose names are a benediction and inspiration to mankind, have been developed, not by soft living and comfortable circumstances, but by hardships, poverty, and persecution. "What went you into the desert to see?" asked Jesus of those who had heard the preaching of John the Baptist. "A reed shaken by the wind? A man clothed in soft garments? Behold those who are clothed in soft garments are in the houses of kings. . . ." Yet this was the man of whom He said, "There hath not risen among them that are born of women a greater. . . . From the days of John the Baptist until now, the kingdom of Heaven suffereth violence and the violent bear it away."[3] St. John suffered martyrdom at the hands of Herod, and Christ Himself calls us up to eternal life with His arms outstretched upon the Cross.

Genuine mastery of life means far more than the elimination of poverty, the advancement of science, and the promotion of health and knowledge. These are of little avail unless supported by a deeper conviction and sense of stability which remain to guide a man's life, even though the material fruits of labor be never at-

---

[2] Matt. 20:22.
[3] Matt. 11:7–12.

tained, or once attained be lost again. The master of life is he who can bear success and misfortune, wealth and poverty, with equal grace and quiet of spirit, not because he is incapable of feeling or embittered against hope, but because he realizes that in the eyes of God nothing else counts except honest effort and generous motive. With divine grace these are within the constant grasp of every man.

Christ, the supreme master of life, accumulated no fortune. His was a life of poverty and persecution. "Blessed," said He, "are the poor in spirit, for theirs is the kingdom of Heaven. . . . Blessed are ye when they shall revile you and persecute you and speak all that is evil against you, untruly for my sake; be glad and rejoice, for your reward is very great in Heaven."[4] Christ teaches a mastery of life that rises above the accidents of fame and fortune, proof against the flattery of prosperity and the despair of failure alike. From His eternal throne as God, He calls to the steady vision of eternity beyond: "Come ye blessed of my Father, possess you the kingdom prepared for you from the foundation of the world."[5]

For those who would learn this mastery of life there is no better offering and prayer than that of St. Ignatius Loyola: "Take, O Lord, and receive all my liberty, my memory, my understanding, and my whole will. Thou hast given me all that I am and all that I possess, I surrender it all to Thee that Thou mayest dispose of it according to Thy will. Give me only Thy love and Thy grace; with these I will be rich, and will have no more to desire."

---

[4] Matt. 5:3, 11, 12.
[5] Matt. 25:34.

II

These considerations are of the utmost importance in our day, which has witnessed every extreme of human fortune. We have seen a world war of staggering proportions, a postwar period of sincere rejoicing amid the groans of the wounded, the mourning of the bereaved, and the revelry of a frenzied generation unaccustomed to peace. From the sinews of war there sprang an era of intoxicating prosperity. Then came a sudden collapse of all the fond dreams of continued expansion. Hunger, discontent, and death again and again stalked the land. Then, as men were gathering courage and seeking security, broke out the second world war. Amid such changes and chaos, thousands of disillusioned men and women are asking themselves whether life has anything that can give repose to the human spirit and offer a worthy motive for renewed effort and rejoicing.

The most unbearable thing in life is continual uncertainty. Even those with every luxury at their command and freedom from worry over health or finances may still be driven to frantic desperation by the boredom of an existence which lacks direction and purpose. The joy of existence can easily vanish from those for whom years of confident toil have ended only in tragic failure. A joyless existence is worse than none at all.

The temptation that comes to people under the strain of financial loss, the death of friends, poor health, disappointment in love, and bitter injustice is the thought that perhaps, after all, there is no guiding principle, no divine Providence, no justice or readjustment possible. The cruelest pessimism is that which regards all as merely the product or chance or as the whim of an unfeeling God.

These thoughts come perhaps to all of us in the presence of death, when we behold youth snatched away in its first flower, while old age smolders along uselessly from season to season. We feel instinctively a process of frustration in the contrast between the rise of ignorant and unworthy people through a stroke of sheer luck and the dismal fall of far abler and more deserving individuals because of some element beyond their control. The Russian novelist, Turgenev, was assailed with this fear of universal confusion as he sat in his garden watching the unequal battle between a toad and a serpent; and in one of his greatest works he pictured the hero as a typical example of his problem, conquering every difficulty of flesh and spirit only to die ingloriously of an insignificant scratch.

However we may look at it, all life and vital activity on earth are certain of only one event in the future, and that is transformation or destruction. The lilies of the field, which Christ beheld as more glorious than the robes of Solomon, have to go the way of all grass. Even though animals and men may issue victorious from any particular conflict, the laws of nature will eventually overtake them in death. The ashes of the world's dead soon lose their identity.

It is useless to deny that, underlying the sorrow, suffering, and disappointments of life, there is a profound mystery. At the same time, is it conceivable that a universe whose most simple operation is governed by physical law, perfection of design, and harmony of cycle should be evolved from utter chaos and should lead nowhere? Can it be that the Great Designer, who has so delicately provided for the lesser things of the universe, should have made no secure or certain provision for man, who is His most noble creation on earth? Is the only law of the human spirit one of blind fate and unintelligent despair?

The beauty and harmony of the universe mean nothing if not that the very imperfections of life have a place in the divine idea. The scroll of human fortune, in God's plan, cannot rest with any particular moment or event. It moves on continuously toward an eternal harmony and readjustment for every individual.

The finest things of life receive their keenest development through this struggle of body and spirit with a hostile environment, and this is the mystery which pessimism has never succeeded in explaining. Sympathy is born in pain and proves itself through faith and sacrifice. Sympathy and appreciation of lasting values grow from intimate contact with suffering. When souls are spared the experience of life's harsher realities, they fail to expand. Lacking the power of deeper imagination, of generosity, which comes from the recollection of a needy period in one's own life, and of tested principle, they fail to grasp the sense of a larger harmony and to feel the fundamental joy of certainty in God's wisdom, particularly during the dark hours of bewilderment and defeat.

It was with realization of this harmony between defeat and triumph, suffering and strength, confusion and certainty, that St. Paul revealed God's answer to his prayer for deliverance: "My grace is sufficient for thee: for power is made perfect in infirmity."[6] After relating the trials and perils of his career for Christ, he

[6] 2 Cor. 12:9.

cried out, as it were, from the house tops: "Who is weak, and I am not weak? Who is scandalized, and I am not on fire? If I must needs glory, I will glory of the things that concern my infirmity."[7] Christ, yearning for the ordeal of the Cross by which He would prove His mission of Redemption, said: "I have a baptism wherewith I am to be baptized. And how am I straitened until it be accomplished?"[8] What moment of His life gave Him a satisfaction and joy comparable to that of His final agony upon the Cross, when He closed His eyes upon the completed work of His sacrifice?

Christ never preached a shallow optimism. He did not deny the reality of life's imperfection, and He gave no assurance that everything will turn out in this world as we might wish. On the contrary, He began with a recognition of suffering. He traced His program of joy through the progressive development of each soul, from suffering, to God. "He that taketh not up his cross and followeth me," He said, "is not worthy of me."[9] For those who have the courage to face life in its entirety, He declared: "My yoke is sweet, and my burden light."[10] Even when all earthly hopes are swept from our grasp, the clear voice of Christ rings out with spiritual joy and encouragement: "Peace I leave with you: My peace I give unto you: not as the world giveth. Let not your heart be troubled: nor let it be afraid."[11]

This reconciliation of self with the divine plan and this constant aspiration for spiritual identification of self with the purposes of God, come what may, are at the root of all successful living. Without this outlook,

---

[7] 2 Cor. 11:29, 30.
[8] Luke 12:50.
[9] Matt. 10:38.
[10] Matt. 11:30.
[11] John 14:27.

one sees but half of life and misses the great lessons that come from pain and sacrifice.

For timid souls who have experienced a succession of reverses this realization is not always easy. Nevertheless, the presence of constant forces, of natural laws and stabilizing elements, of beauty and harmony, of the recurrence and the propagation of life in the same highly complex, normally functioning forms; of goodness, and gratitude, and retribution, make a pessimistic view of life untenable. The impact of various forces, on occasion, turns us aside from immediate objectives, and compels us to take detours very much like those on rocky, mountainous roads; but unless our objectives are mistaken ones, they must lead to something consonant with life's great plan, capable of realization and success.

III

If, then, we go one step further, we may reasonably inquire whether there is not some smoothly working plan, some basis or body of rules, for attaining this plan and purpose. In other words, is there such a thing as a practical art of successful living? And, finally, is this art available to everyone?

The answer to these questions, which every person consciously asks at least once during his lifetime, depends on the objective he has in mind, his standard of values, and his concept of success. If, for example, one were to propose the accumulation of one million dollars, or even a considerable fraction of that amount, as the standard of success in life, obviously most men and women would be leading unsuccessful lives. Even a brave attempt to reach this goal could not in itself characterize what might be called a successful life. The mere output of energy and toil, as such, has no special human value apart from the motive that accompanies it; and life's meaning can hardly be restricted to the accumulation, real or attempted, of material goods.

One of the great mistakes made through the ages, however, has been this glorification of material necessities and conveniences to a point where they become an end in themselves – the badge of successful living. As a result of opportunities in our own country, the successful man is rather generally regarded as one who has made money and wielded power. The man whose home, clothes, car, club, social standing, and financial rating are the envy of those upon whom fortune has smiled more faintly thus becomes the paragon and ideal of success.

Acquisitions of this kind may, and often do, represent sterling qualities of labor, thrift, and perseverance that may well be held up for the admiration and imitation of youth. But these qualities, in pursuit of merely material ends, can be thwarted by bad luck involving elements beyond our control, as many a businessman or investor has learned bitterly within these past few years. On the other hand, wealth and its favors can be the reward of crime and graft, of cutthroat competition, and of those sundry malpractices that threaten to disrupt the social order. Possession of the fat of the land does not necessarily indicate a successful life in the complete, enduring sense.

Reaction against this standard of success, however, is not immune from falling into equally unhappy ideas of a successful life. In fact, the sudden loss of money in investments and a feeling of financial insecurity in many cases have led people to think that rapid and riotous spending of available funds is the answer to success. The current expression "You can't take it with you" conveys this idea of futility, but with no substitute except that of pleasure.

Undoubtedly, a great deal of the publicized frivolity that mars American life is due to this feeling of personal frustration – the lack of a sense of direction or of final values. As a result of this unfortunate point of view, the personal and immediate satisfaction of the individual becomes the only measure of success. The establishment of a home, the rearing of a family, and the acceptance of those responsibilities and sacrifices that these tasks entail are rejected from sheerly selfish motives; and the sole object in life becomes that of squeezing as much agreeable sensation from the moment as possible. The dissipation and utter lack of constructive or social contribution in this outlook eliminate it, without further question, from serious claim to successful living.

The young man who approached Christ had undoubtedly given thought to these considerations when he asked: "Good Master, what good shall I do that I may have life everlasting?" Jesus answered: "Keep the commandments. . . . Thou shalt do no murder. Thou shalt not commit adultery. Thou shalt not steal. Thou shalt not bear false witness. . . . Thou shalt love thy neighbor as thyself." The young man was still unsatisfied. "All these," he replied, "have I kept from my youth. What is yet wanting to me?" And then the Master said that which sent the young man away sad: "If thou wilt be perfect, go sell what thou hast and give to the poor and thou shalt have treasure in heaven. And come follow me."[12]

The terms of success which Christ laid down on this occasion do not, it is true, lend themselves to a literal carrying out by the rank and file of men and women. Nor does the career of Christ, particularly with its culmination on the Cross, seem to spell success, if immediate, social recognition and gratitude are the first signs of masterful living. Still, in the full and complete meaning of the word, Jesus has given the only true standard and measure of success.

In the first place, He gives a finality to life. "One is good," He says, "God."[13] He outlines the means by which life's purpose is unfolded and fulfilled – the keeping of the Commandments, not as a detached act or intention, but as the mold and direction of daily life. And the measure of success He indicates as the degree in which each individual has striven to give of himself for the goodness and happiness and final salvation of others – even with self-sacrifice, and all this for the supreme purpose of the love of God.

Can this be called a progressive art? Undoubtedly it can, for it involves the special talents and powers of each individual, and requires careful application in definite fields of activity. Christ expressed Himself perfectly on this point in His parable of the talents and the three servants to whom they were confided. Two of the men improved what they had and showed a gain in their use. But the third, who hid his talent in a napkin (for he was afraid, so he said, that he

---

[12] Matt. 19:16–21.
[13] Matt. 19:17.

might lose it in an investment) received a rebuke from the Master. The use of our talents and powers in the generous service of others never dims their brilliance or leaves us in want. On the contrary, we learn by teaching, we receive by giving, we gain by thoughtful sacrifice. Success is never gained by selfishness. Not what one has, but what one gives, is the measure of achievement and enduring appreciation.

The history of true success has been precisely this; and the gratitude of the world and the special reward bestowed by God are ready for those who have improved themselves that they may have more to give in the service of others. Recognition may sometimes be slow and even late, but where true value exists, there is success. Upon the Cross, Christ stands as an eternal rebuke to those whose lives are muffled in the selfishness of fear lest men impose on them, and as an eternal inspiration in the fine art of successful living — the Mastery of Life.

INDEX